INFANT BAPTISM
Scriptural and Reasonable

with

Baptism By Sprinkling or Affusion the Most Suitable and Edifying Mode

In Four Discourses

by
Samuel Miller, D.D.
Professor of Ecclesiastical History and Church Government
in the Theological Seminary at Princeton

sola fide
PUBLISHERS

www.solafidepublishers.com

Infant Baptism
Scriptural and Reasonable
by Samuel Miller

Originally Published in 1835
by Joseph Whetham
Philadelphia

Reprint Edition © 2015
Sola Fide Publishers
Post Office Box 2027
Toccoa, Georgia 30577
www.solafidepublishers.com

Cover and Interior Design by
Magnolia Graphic Design
www.magnoliagraphicdesign.com

ISBN-13: 978-0692569016
ISBN-10: 0692569014

CONTENTS

INTRODUCTION

The substance of the following discourses was delivered, in two sermons, in the church in Freehold, Monmouth county, New Jersey, on the 29th of September, 1833. A desire for their publication having been expressed by some who heard them, I have thought proper to revise and enlarge the whole, and present it in the present form. The subject is one which has given rise to much warm discussion, and it would seem, at first view, to be a work of supererogation, if not of still more unfavourable character, to trouble the Christian community with another treatise upon it. But our Antipædobaptist brethren appear to be resolved that it shall never cease to be agitated; and as, indeed, the constant stirring of this controversy seems to furnish no small share of the very aliment on which they depend for subsistence as a denomination, they cannot be expected to let it rest. The great importance of the subject, in my estimation, and the hope that this little volume may reach and benefit some, who are in danger of being drawn into the toils of error, and have no opportunity of perusing larger works, have induced me to undergo the labour of preparing it for the press.

My object is, not to write for the learned, but to present the subject in that brief, plain, popular manner which is adapted to the case of those who read but little. I have, therefore, designedly avoided the introduction of much matter which properly belongs to the subject, and which is to be found in larger treatises; and have especially refrained from entering further into the field of philological discussion, than was absolutely necessary for

5

the accomplishment of my plan.

If I know my own heart, my purpose is, not to wound the feelings of a human being – not to stir up strife – but to provide a little manual, better adapted than any *of this class* that I have seen, for the use of those Presbyterians who are continually assaulted, and sometimes perplexed, by their Baptist neighbours. May the Divine benediction rest upon the humble offering!

Samuel Miller
Princeton, Nov. 1834.

CHAPTER ONE

Infant Baptism Established

"And when she was baptized, and her household, she besought us, saying, if ye have judged me to be faithful to the Lord, come into mine house and abide there" (Acts xvi.15).

As man has a body as well as a soul, so it has pleased infinite wisdom to appoint something in religion adapted to both parts of our nature. Something to strike the senses, as well as to impress the conscience and the heart; or rather, something which might, through the medium of the senses, reach and benefit the spiritual part of our constitution. For, as our bodies, in this world of sin and death, often become sources of moral mischief and pain, so, by the grace of God, they are made inlets to the most refined moral pleasures, and means of advancement in the divine life.

But while the outward senses are to be consulted in religion, they are not to be invested with unlimited dominion. Accordingly the external rites and ceremonies of Christianity are few and simple, but exceedingly appropriate and significant. We have but two sacraments, the one emblematical of that spiritual cleansing, and the other of that spiritual nourishment, which we need both for enjoyment and for duty. To one of these sacramental ordinances there is a pointed reference in the original commission given by their Master to the apostles: "Go ye into all the world, and preach the Gospel to every creature, – baptizing them in the name of the Father, and of the Son, and of the Holy Ghost; teaching them to observe all things whatsoever I have commanded you, and lo, I am with you always, even unto the end of the world" (Matt. xxviii. 19, 20). And, accordingly, wherever the Gospel was received, we find holy baptism reverently administered as a sign and seal of membership in the family of Christ. Thus on the occasion to which our text refers, "a certain woman," We are told, "named Lydia, a seller of purple, of the city of Thyatira, heard Paul and Silas preach in the city of Philippi; and the Lord opened her heart, so that she attended unto the things which were spoken of Paul. And when she was baptized, and her household, she besought us, saying, If ye have judged me to be faithful to the Lord, come into mine house and abide there."

I propose, my friends, from these words, to address you on the subject of *Christian baptism.* You are sensible that this is a subject on which much controversy has existed, in modern times, among professing Christians. It shall be my endeavour, by the grace of God, with all candour and impartiality, to inquire what the Scriptures teach concerning this ordinance, and what appears to have been the practice in regard to it in the purest and best ages of the Christian Church, as well as in later times. May I be enabled to speak, and you to hear as becomes those who expect, in a little while, to stand before the judgment seat of Christ.

There are two questions concerning baptism to which I request your special attention at this time, viz: Who are the *proper subjects* of this ordinance? And in *what manner* ought it to be administered? To the first of these questions our attention will be directed in the present, and the ensuing discourse.

I. Who are to be considered as *the proper subjects of Christian baptism?*

That baptism ought to be administered to all adult persons, who profess faith in Christ, and obedience to him, and who have not been baptized in their infancy, is not doubted by any. In this all who consider baptism as an ordinance at present obligatory are agreed. But it is well known that there is a large and respectable body of professing Christians among us who believe, and confidently assert, that baptism ought to be confined to adults; who insist, that when professing Christians bring their infant offspring, and dedicate them to God, and receive for them the washing of sacramental water in the name of the Father, and of the Son, and of the Holy Ghost, they entirely pervert and misapply an important Christian ordinance. We highly respect the sincerity and piety of many who entertain these opinions; but we are perfectly persuaded that they are in error, nay in great and mischievous error; an error which cannot fail of exerting a most unhappy influence on the best interests of the Church of God. We have no doubt that the visible Church is made up, not only of those who personally profess the true religion, but also of their children; and that we are bound not only to confess Christ before men for ourselves, but also to bring our infant seed in the arms of faith and love, and present them before the Lord, in that ordinance which is at once a seal of God's covenant with His people, and an emblem of those spiritual blessings which, as sinners, we and our children equally and indispensably need.

Our reasons for entertaining this opinion, with entire confidence, are the following:

1. Because *in all Jehovah's covenants with His professing people, from the earliest ages, and in all states of society, their infant seed have been included.* That this was the case with regard to the first covenant made with Adam in paradise, is granted by all; certainly by all with whom we have any controversy concerning infant baptism. And, indeed, the consequences of the violation of that covenant, to all his posterity, furnish a standing and a mournful testimony that it embraced them all. The covenant made with Noah, after the deluge, was, as to this point, of the same character. Its language was, "Behold, I establish my covenant with thee and with thy *seed.*" The covenant with Abraham was equally comprehensive. "Behold," says Jehovah, "my covenant is with thee, Behold, I establish my covenant with thee, and with thy *seed,* after thee." The covenants of Sinai and of Moab,

it is evident, also comprehended the children of the immediate actors in the passing scenes, and attached to them, as well as to their fathers, an interest in blessings or the curses, the promises or the threatenings which those covenants respectively included. Accordingly when Moses was about to take leave of the people, he addressed them as "standing before the Lord their God, with their little ones, and their wives, to enter into covenant with the Lord their God" (Deut. xxix. 10-12). And when we come to the New Testament economy, still we find the same interesting feature not only retained, but more strikingly and strongly displayed. Still the promise, it is declared, is "to us and our children, even as many as the Lord our God shall call."

Now, has this been a feature in all Jehovah's covenants with His people in every age? And shall we admit the idea of its failing in that New Testament or Christian covenant, which, though the same in substance with those which preceded it, excels them all in the extent of its privileges, and in the glory of its promises? It cannot be. The thought is inadmissible. But further,

2. The *close and endearing connection between parents and children* affords a strong argument in favour of the church membership of the infant seed of believers. The voice of nature is lifted up, and pleads most powerfully in behalf of our cause. The thought of severing parents from their offspring, in regard to the most interesting relations in which it has pleased God in His adorable providence to place them, is equally repugnant to Christian feeling, and to natural law. Can it be, my friends, that when the stem is in the Church, the branch is out of it? Can it be that when the parent is within the visible kingdom of the Redeemer, his offspring, bone of his bone, and flesh of his flesh, have no connection with it? It is not so in any other society that the great moral Governor of the world ever formed. It is not so in civil society. Children are born citizens of the State in which their parents resided at the time of their birth. In virtue of their birth they are plenary citizens, bound by all the duties, and entitled to all the privileges of that relation, whenever they become capable of exercising them. From these duties they cannot be liberated. Of

these privileges they cannot be deprived, but by the commission of crime. But why should this great principle be set aside in the Church of God? Surely it is not less obvious or less powerful in grace than in nature. The analogies which pervade all the works and dispensations of God are too uniform and striking to be disregarded in an inquiry like the present. But we hasten to facts and considerations still more explicitly laid down in Holy Scripture.

3. *The actual and acknowledged church membership of infants under the Old Testament economy,* is a decisive index of the Divine will in regard to this matter.

Whatever else may be doubtful, it is certain that infants were, in fact, members of the Church under the former dispensation; and, as such, were the regular subjects of a covenant seal. When God called Abraham, and established His covenant with him, He not only embraced his infant seed, in the most express terms, in that covenant, but He also appointed an ordinance by which this relation of his children to the visible Church was publicly ratified and sealed, and that when they were only eight days old. If Jewish adults were members of the Church of God, under that economy, then, assuredly, their infant seed were equally members, for they were brought into the same covenant relation, and had the same covenant seal impressed upon their flesh as their adult parents. This covenant, moreover, had a respect to spiritual as well as temporal blessings. Circumcision is expressly declared, by the inspired apostle, to have been "a seal of the righteousness of faith" (Rom. iv. 11). So far was it from being a mere pledge of the possession of Canaan, and the enjoyment of temporal prosperity there, that it ratified and sealed a covenant in which "all the families of the earth were to be blessed." And yet this covenant seal was solemnly appointed by God to be administered, and was actually administered, for nearly two thousand years, to infants of the tenderest age, in token of their relation to God's covenanted family, and of their right to the privileges of that covenant. Here, then, is a *fact,* – a fact incapable of being disguised or denied, – nay, a fact acknowledged by all – on which the advocates of infant baptism may stand as upon an immoveable rock.

For if infinite wisdom once saw that it was right and fit that infants should be made the subjects of "a seal of the righteousness of faith," before they were capable of exercising faith, surely a transaction the same in substance may be right and fit now. Baptism, which is, in like manner, a seal of the righteousness of faith, may, without impropriety, be applied equally early. What once, undoubtedly, existed in the Church, and that by Divine appointment, may exist still, without any impeachment of either the wisdom or benevolence of Him who appointed it. But,

4. As the infant seed of the people of God are acknowledged on all hands to have been members of the Church, equally with their parents, under the Old Testament dispensation, *so it is equally certain that the Church of God is the same in substance now that it was then;* and, of course, it is just as reasonable and proper, on principle, that the infant offspring of professed believers should be members of the Church now, as it was that they should be members of the ancient Church. I am aware that our Baptist brethren warmly object to this statement, and assert that the Church of God under the Old Testament economy and the New, is not the same, but so essentially different, that the same principles can by no means apply to each. They contend that the Old Testament dispensation was a kind of political economy, rather national than spiritual in its character; and, of course, that when the Jews ceased to be a people, the covenant under which they had been placed, was altogether laid aside, and a covenant of an entirely new character introduced. But nothing can be more evident than that this view of the subject is entirely erroneous. The perpetuity of the Abrahamic covenant, and, of consequence, the identity of the Church under both dispensations, is so plainly taught in Scripture, and follows so unavoidably from the radical scriptural principles concerning the Church of God, that it is indeed wonderful how any believer in the Bible can call in question the fact. Every thing essential to ecclesiastical identity is evidently found here. The same Divine Head; the same precious covenant; the same great spiritual design; the same atoning blood; the same sanctifying Spirit, in which we rejoice, as the life and the glory of

the New Testament Church, we know, from the testimony of Scripture, were also the life and the glory of the Church before the coming of the Messiah. It is not more certain that a man, arrived at mature age, is the same individual that he was when an infant on his mother's lap, than it is that the Church, in the plenitude of her light and privileges, after the coming of Christ, is the same Church which, many centuries before, though with a much smaller amount of light and privilege, yet, as we are expressly told in the New Testament, enjoyed the presence and guidance of her divine Head "in the wilderness" (Acts vii. 38). The truth is, the inspired apostle, in writing to the Galatians, formally compares the covenanted people of God, under the Old Testament economy, to an heir under age: "Now I say, that the heir, as long as he is a child, differeth nothing from a servant, though he be lord of all; but is under tutors and governors, until the time appointed of the father. Even so we, when we were children, were in bondage under the elements of the world. But when the fulness of the time was come, God sent forth His Son, made of a woman, made under the law, to redeem them that were under the law, that we might receive the adoption of sons" (iv. 1-6).

Hence, the inspired apostle, in writing to the Hebrews, referring to the children of Israel, says: "Unto us was the Gospel preached, as well as unto them" (iv. 2). Again, in writing to the Corinthians, he declares, "They did all eat the same spiritual meat, and did all drink the same spiritual drink; for they drank of that spiritual rock which followed them, and that rock was Christ" (x. 1-4). "Abraham," we are told, "rejoiced to see Christ's day; he saw it, and was glad" (John viii. 56). And, of the patriarchs generally, we are assured that they saw Gospel promises afar off, and embraced them. The Church under the old economy, then, was not only a church – a true church – a divinely constituted church – but it was a Gospel church, a church of Christ – a church built upon the "same foundation as that of the apostles."

But what places the identity of the Church, under both dispensations, in the clearest and strongest light, is that memorable and decisive passage, in the 11th chapter of the epistle to the

Romans, in which the Church of God is held forth to us under the emblem of an olive tree. Under the same figure had the Lord designated the Church by the pen of Jeremiah the prophet, in the 11th chapter of his prophecy. The prophet, speaking of God's covenanted people under that economy, says: "The Lord called thy name a green olive tree, *fair* and of goodly *fruit.*" But concerning this olive tree, on account of the sin of the people in forsaking the Lord, the prophet declares: "With the noise of a great tumult he hath kindled a fire upon it, and the branches of it are broken." Let me request you to compare with this, the language of the apostle in the 11th chapter of the epistle to the Romans: "For if the casting away of them be the reconciling of the world, what shall the receiving of them be but life from the dead? For if the first fruit be holy, the lump is also holy; and if the root be holy, so are the branches. And if some of the branches be broken off; and thou, being a wild olive tree, wert grafted in among them, and with them partakest of the root and fatness of the olive tree; boast not against the branches; but if thou boast, thou bearest not the root, but the root thee. Thou wilt say, then, the branches were broken off, that I might be grafted in. Well, because of unbelief they were broken off, and thou standest by faith. Be not high-minded, but fear. For if God spared not the natural branches, take heed lest he also spare not thee. Behold, therefore, the goodness and the severity of God! on them which fell severity; but toward thee goodness, if thou continue in His goodness. Otherwise, thou also shalt be broken off. And they also, if they abide not still in unbelief, shall be grafted in, for God is able to graft them in *again.* For if thou wert cut out of the olive tree, which is wild by nature, and wert grafted contrary to nature, into a good olive tree, how much more shall these, which be the natural branches, be grafted into their own olive tree?"

That the apostle is here speaking of the Old Testament Church, under the figure of a good olive tree, cannot be doubted, and is, indeed, acknowledged by all; by our Baptist brethren as well as others. Now the inspired apostle says concerning this olive tree, that the natural branches – that is the Jews – were broken off because of unbelief. But what was the consequence of this excision? Was the tree destroyed? By no means. The apostle teaches directly the contrary. It is evident, from his language, that the root and trunk, in all their "fatness," remained; and Gentiles, branches of an olive tree "wild by nature," were "grafted into the good olive tree;" – the *same tree* from which the natural branches had been broken *off.* Can any thing be more pointedly descriptive of *identity* than this? But this is not all. The apostle apprizes us that the Jews are to be brought back from their rebellion and wanderings, and to be incorporated with the Christian Church. And how is this restoration described? It is called "grafting them in *again into their own olive tree."* In other words, the "tree" into which the Gentile Christians, at the coming of Christ were "grafted," was the "old olive tree," of which the ancient covenant people of God were the "natural branches;" and, of course, when the Jews shall be brought in, with the fulness of the Gentiles, into the Christian Church, the apostle expressly tells us they shall be *"grafted in again to their own olive tree."* Surely, if the Church of God before the coming of Christ, and the Church of God after the advent, were altogether distinct and separate bodies, and not the same in their essential characters, it would be an abuse of terms to represent the Jews, when converted to Christianity, as *grafted in again into their own olive tree.*

5. Having seen that the infant seed of the professing people of God *were* members of the Church under the Old Testament economy; and having seen also that the Church under that dispensation and the present is *the same;* we are evidently prepared to take another step, and to infer, that, *if infants were once members, and if the Church remains the same, they undoubtedly are still members, unless some positive divine enactment excluding them, can be found.* As it was a positive divine enactment which brought them in, and gave them a place in the Church, so it is evident that a divine enactment as direct and positive, repealing their old privilege, and excluding them from the covenanted family, must be found, or they are still in the Church. But can such an act of repeal and exclusion, I ask, be produced? It cannot. It

never has been, and it never can be. The introduction of infants into the Church by divine appointment, is undoubted. The identity of the Church, under both dispensations, is undoubted. The perpetuity of the Abrahamic covenant, in which not merely the lineal descendants of Abraham, but *"all the nations of the earth were to be blessed,"* is undoubted. And we find no hint in the New Testament of the high privilege granted to the infant seed of believers being withdrawn. Only concede that it has not been formally withdrawn, and it remains of course. The advocates of infant baptism are not bound to produce from the New Testament an express warrant for the membership of the children of believers. The warrant was given, most expressly and formally, two thousand years before the New Testament was written; and, having never been revoked, remains firmly and indisputably in force.

It is deeply to be lamented that our Baptist brethren cannot be prevailed upon to recognise the length and breadth, and bearing of this great ecclesiastical fact. Here were little children, eight days old, acknowledged as members of a covenanted society – a society consecrated to God, for spiritual as well as temporal benefits – and stamped with a covenant seal, by which they were formally bound, as the seed of believers, to be entirely and forever the Lord's. Can infant membership be ridiculed, as it often is, without lifting the puny arm against Him who was with "his church in the wilderness, and whose ways are all wise and righteous"?

6. Our next step is to *show that baptism, has come in the room of circumcision,* and, therefore, that the former is rightfully and properly applied to the same subjects as the latter. When we say this, we mean, not merely that circumcision is laid aside in the Church of Christ, and that baptism has been brought in, but that baptism occupies the same place, as the appointed initiatory ordinance in the Church, and that, as a moral emblem, it means the same thing. The meaning and design of circumcision was chiefly spiritual. It was a seal of a covenant which had not solely, or even mainly, a respect to the possession of Canaan, and to the temporal promises which were connected with a residence in that land;

but which chiefly regarded higher and more important blessings, even those which are conveyed through the Messiah, in
whom "all the families of the earth" are to be blessed. So it
is with baptism. While it marks an external relation, and seals
outward privileges, it is, as circumcision was, a "seal of the
righteousness of faith," and has a primary reference to the
benefits of the Messiah's mission and reign. Circumcision
was a token of visible membership in the family of God, and
of covenant obligation to Him. So is baptism. Circumcision
was the ordinance which marked, or publicly ratified, entrance into that visible family. So does baptism. Circumcision
was an emblem of moral cleansing and purity. So is baptism.
It refers to the remission of sins by the blood of Christ, and
regeneration by His Spirit; and teaches us that we are by
nature guilty and depraved, and stand in need of the pardoning and sanctifying grace of God by a crucified Redeemer.
Surely, then, there is the best foundation for asserting that
baptism has come in the place of circumcision. The latter, as
all grant, has been discontinued; and now baptism occupies
the same place, means the same thing, seals the same covenant, and is a pledge of the same spiritual blessings. Who can
doubt, then, that there is the utmost propriety, upon principle, in applying it to the same infant subjects?

Yet, though baptism manifestly comes in the place of
circumcision, there are points in regard to which the former
differs materially from the latter. And it differs precisely as
to those points in regard to which the New Testament economy differs from the Old, in being more enlarged, and less
ceremonial. Baptism is not ceremonially restricted to the
eighth day, but may be administered at any time and place.
It is not confined to one sex; but, like the glorious dispensation of which it is a seal, it marks an enlarged privilege, and
is administered in a way which reminds us, that "there is neither Greek nor Jew, neither bond nor free, neither male nor
female, in the Christian economy; but that we are all one in
Christ Jesus."

7. Again; it is a strong argument in favour of infant baptism, that *we find the principle of family baptism again and again adopted in the apostolic age.* We are told, by men learned in Jewish antiquities, that, under the Old Testament economy, it was customary, when proselytes to Judaism were gained from the surrounding nations, that all the children of a family were invariably admitted to membership in the Church with their parents, and on the faith of their parents; that all the males, children and adults, were circumcised, and the whole family, male and female, baptized, and incorporated with the community of God's covenanted people.[1] Accordingly, when we examine the New Testament history, we find that, under the ministry of the apostles, who were all native Jews, and had, of course, been long accustomed to this practice, the same principle of receiving and baptizing families on the faith of the parents, was most evidently adopted and acted upon in a very striking manner. When "the heart of Lydia was opened, so that she attended to the things which were spoken by Paul," we are told that "she was baptized and her household." When the jailor at Philippi believed, "he was baptized, he and all his, straightway." Thus also we read of "the household of Stephanas" being baptized. Now, though we are not certain that there were young children in any of these families, it is highly probable there were. At any rate, the great principle of *family baptism,* of receiving all the younger members of house-

---

1. I consider the Jewish baptism of proselytes as a historical fact well established. I am aware that some Pædobaptists, whose judgment and learning I greatly respect, have expressed doubts in reference to this matter. But when I find the Jews asking John the Baptist, "Why baptizest thou, then, if thou be not the Christ?" &c., I can only account for their language by supposing that they had been accustomed to that rite, and expected the Messiah, when He came, to practice it. We have the best evidence that they baptized their proselytes as early as the second century; and it is altogether incredible that they should copy it from the Christians. And a great majority of the most competent judges in this case, both Jewish and Christian, from Selden and Lightfoot down to Dr. Adam Clarke, have considered the testimony to the fact as abundant and conclusive.

holds *on the faith of their domestic head,* seems to be plainly and decisively established. This furnishes ground on which the advocate of infant baptism may stand with unwavering confidence.

And here let me ask, was it ever known that a case of family baptism occurred under the direction of a Baptist minister? Was it ever known to be recorded, or to have happened, that when, under the influence of Baptist ministrations, the parents of large families were hopefully converted, they were baptized, they and all their's straightway? There is no risk in asserting that such a case was never heard of. And why? Evidently, because our Baptist brethren do not act in this matter upon the principles laid down in the New Testament, and which regulated the primitive Christians.

8. Another consideration possesses much weight here. We cannot imagine that the privileges and the sign of infant membership, to which all the first Christians had been so long accustomed, could have been abruptly withdrawn, *without wounding the hearts of parents, and producing in them feelings of deep revolt and complaint against the new economy.* Yet we find no hint of this recorded in the history of the apostolic age. Upon our principles, this entire silence presents no difficulty. The old principle and practice of infant membership, so long consecrated by time, and so dear to all the feelings of parental affection, went on as before. The identity of the Church under the new dispensation with that of the old, being well understood, the early Christians needed no new warrant for the inclusion of their infant seed in the covenanted family. As the privilege had not been revoked, it, of course, continued. A new and formal enactment in favour of the privilege would have been altogether superfluous, not to say out of place; especially as it was well understood, from the whole aspect of the new economy, that, instead of withdrawing or narrowing privileges, its whole character was that it rather multiplied and extended them.

But our Baptist brethren are under the necessity of supposing, that such of the first Christians as had been Jews, and who had ever been in the habit of considering their beloved off-

spring as included, with themselves, in the privileges and promises of God's covenant, were given to understand, when the New
Testament Church was set up, that these covenant privileges and
promises were no longer to be enjoyed by their children; that they
were, henceforth, to be no more connected with the Church than
the children of the surrounding heathen; and this under an economy distinguished, in every other respect, by greater light, and
more enlarged privilege: – I say, our Baptist brethren are under
the necessity of supposing that the first Christians were met on
the organization of the New Testament Church, with an an-
nouncement of this kind, and that they acquiesced in it without a
feeling of surprise, or a word of murmur! Nay, that this whole
retrograde change passed with so little feeling of interest, that it
was never so much as mentioned or hinted at in any of the epistles to the churches. But can this supposition be for a moment
admitted? It is impossible. We may conclude, then, that the acknowledged silence of the New Testament as to any retraction of
the old privileges, or any complaint of its recall, is so far from
warranting a conclusion unfavourable to the church membership
of infants, that it furnishes a weighty argument of an import directly the reverse.

9. Although the New Testament does not contain any
specific texts, which, in so many words, declare that the infant
seed of believers are members of the Church in virtue of their
birth; yet *it abounds in passages which cannot reasonably be
explained but in harmony with this doctrine.* The following are
a specimen of the passages to which I refer.

The prophet Isaiah, though not a New Testament writer,
speaks much, and in the most interesting manner, of the New
Testament times. Speaking of the "latter day glory," of that day
when "the wolf and the lamb shall feed together, and the lion shall
eat straw like the bullock, and when there shall be nothing to hurt
or destroy in all God's holy mountain;" speaking of that day, the
inspired prophet declares, "Behold, I create new heavens, and a
new earth, and the former shall not be remembered, nor come
into mind. For as the days of a tree are the days of my people,

and mine elect shall long enjoy the work of their hands. They shall not labour in vain, nor bring forth for trouble; for they are the seed of the blessed of the Lord, *and their offspring with them"* (Isaiah lxv. 17:22, 23).

The language of our Lord concerning little children can be reconciled with no other doctrine than that which I am now endeavouring to establish: "Then were there brought unto him little children, that he should put his hands on them and pray; and His disciples rebuked them. But Jesus said, 'Suffer little children to come unto me, and forbid them not, for of such is the kingdom of heaven.' And he laid his hands upon them, and departed thence" (Matt. xix. 13-15). On examining the language used by the several Evangelists in regard to this occurrence, it is evident that the children here spoken of were young children, infants, such as the Saviour could "take in his arms." The language which our Lord Himself employs concerning them is remarkable. "Of such is the kingdom of heaven." That is, theirs is the kingdom of heaven; or, to them belongs the kingdom of heaven. It is precisely the same form of expression, in the original, which our Lord uses in the commencement of His sermon on the mount, when He says, "Blessed are the poor in spirit, for theirs is the kingdom of heaven," "Blessed are they that are persecuted for righteousness sake, for theirs is the kingdom of heaven." This form of expression, of course, precludes the construction which some have been disposed to put on the passage, in order to evade its force, viz, that it implies, that the kingdom of heaven is made up of such as resemble little children in spirit. We might just as well say, that the kingdom of heaven does not belong to those who are "poor in spirit," but only to those who resemble them; or, that it does not belong to those who are "persecuted for righteousness sake," but only to those who manifest a similar temper. Our Lord's language undoubtedly meant that the kingdom of heaven was really theirs of whom He spake; that it belonged to them; that they are the heirs of it, just as the "poor in spirit," and the "persecuted for righteousness sake," are themselves connected in spirit and in promise with that kingdom.

But what are we to understand by the phrase "the kingdom of heaven," as employed in this place? Most manifestly, we are to understand by it, the visible Church, or the visible kingdom of Christ, as distinguished both from the world, and the old economy. Let any one impartially examine the Evangelists throughout, and he will find this to be the general import of the phrase in question. If this be the meaning, then our Saviour asserts, in the most direct and pointed terms, the reality and the Divine warrant of infant church membership. But *even if* the kingdom of glory be intended, still our argument is not weakened, but rather fortified. For if the kingdom of glory belong to the infant *seed* of believers, much more have they a title to the privileges of the Church on earth.

Another passage of Scripture strongly speaks the same language. I refer to the declaration which we find in the sermon of the apostle Peter, on the day of Pentecost. When a large number of the hearers, on that solemn day, were "pricked in their hearts, and said unto Peter, and to the rest of the apostles, men and brethren, what shall we do?" The reply of the inspired minister of Christ was, "Repent, and be baptized, every one of you, in the name of Jesus Christ, for the remission of sins, and ye shall receive the gift of the Holy Ghost. *For the promise is unto you, and to your children,* and to all that are afar off, even as many as the Lord our God shall call." The apostle is here evidently speaking of the promise of God to His covenant people; that promise in which He engages to be their God, and to constitute them His covenanted family. Now this promise, he declared to those whom he addressed, extended to their children as well as to themselves, and, of course, gave those children a covenant right to the privileges of the family. But if they have a covenant title to a place in this family, we need no formal argument to show that they are entitled to the outward token and seal of that family.

I shall adduce only one more passage of Scripture, at present, in support of the doctrine for which I contend. I refer to that remarkable, and, as it appears to me, conclusive declaration of the apostle Paul, concerning children, which is found in the seventh chapter of the first Epistle to the Corinthians, in reply to a query addressed to him by the members of that church, respecting the Christian law of marriage: "The unbelieving husband is sanctified by the wife; and the unbelieving wife is sanctified by the husband; else were your children unclean, but now are they holy." The great question in relation to this passage is, in what sense does a believing parent "sanctify" an unbelieving one, so that their children are "holy"? It certainly cannot mean, that every pious husband or wife that is allied to an unbelieving partner, is always instrumental in conferring on that partner true spiritual purity, or, in other words, regeneration and sanctification of heart; nor that every child born of parents of whom one is a believer, is, of course, the subject of Gospel holiness, or of internal sanctification. No one who intelligently reads the Bible, or who has eyes to see what daily passes around him, can possibly put such a construction on the passage. Neither can it be understood to mean, as some have strangely imagined, that where one of the parents is a believer, the children are legitimate; that is, the offspring of parents, one of whom is pious, are no longer bastards, but are to be considered as begotten in lawful wedlock! The word "holy" is no where applied in Scripture to legitimacy of birth. The advocates of this construction may be challenged to produce a single example of such an application of the term. And as to the suggestion of piety in one party being necessary to render a marriage covenant valid, nothing can be more absurd. Were the marriages of the heathen in the days of Paul all illicit connections? Are the matrimonial contracts which take place every day, among us, where neither of the parties is pious, all illegitimate and invalid? Surely it is not easy to conceive of a subterfuge more completely preposterous, or more adapted to discredit a cause which finds it necessary to resort to such aid.

The terms "holy" and "unclean," as is well known to all attentive readers of Scripture, have not only a spiritual, but also an ecclesiastical sense, in the Word of God. While, in some eases, they express that which is internally and spiritually conformed to the Divine image; in others, they quite as plainly designate something set apart to a holy or sacred use; that is, separated from a common or profane, to a holy purpose. Thus, under the Old Testament economy, the peculiar people of God, are said to be a "holy people," and to be "severed from all other people, that they might be the Lord's;" not because they were all, or even a majority of them, really consecrated in heart to God; but because they were all His professing people, – His covenanted people; they all belonged to that external body which He had called out of the world, and established as the depository of His truth, and the conservator of His glory. In these two senses, the terms "holy" and "unclean" are used in both Testaments' times, almost innumerable. And what their meaning is, in any particular case, must be gathered from the scope of the passage. In the case before us, the latter of these two senses is evidently required by the whole spirit of the apostle's reasoning.

It appears that among the Corinthians, to whom the apostle wrote, there were many cases of professing Christians being united by the marriage tie with pagans; the former, perhaps, being converted after marriage; or being so unwise, as, after conversion, deliberately to form this unequal and unhappy connection. What was to be deemed of such marriages, seems to have been the grave question submitted to this inspired teacher. He pronounces, under the direction of the Holy Spirit, that, in all such cases, when the unbeliever is willing to live with the believer, they ought to continue to live together; that their connection is so sanctified by the character of the believing companion, that their children are "holy," that is, in covenant with God; members of that church with which the believing parent is, in virtue of his profession, united: in one word, that the infidel party is so far, and in such a sense, consecrated by the believing party, that their children shall be reckoned to belong to the sacred family with which the latter is connected, and shall be regarded and treated as members of the Church of God.[2]

"The passage thus explained," says an able writer, "establishes the church membership of infants in another form. For it assumes the principle, that when both parents are reputed believers, their children belong to the Church of God as a matter of course. The whole difficulty proposed by the Corinthians to Paul, grows out of this principle. Had he taught, or they understood, that no children, be their parents believers or unbelievers, are to be accounted members of the Church, the difficulty could not have existed. For if the faith of both parents could not confer upon the child the privilege of membership, the faith of only one of them certainly could not. The point was decided. It would have been mere impertinence to teaze the apostle with queries which carried their own answers along with them. But on the supposition that when both parents were members, their children were also members; the difficulty is very natural and serious. 'I see,' would a Corinthian convert exclaim, 'I see the children of my Christian neighbours, owned as members of the Church of God; and I see the children of others, who are unbelievers, rejected with themselves. I believe in Christ myself: but my husband, my wife, believes not. What is to become of my children? Are they to be admitted with myself? Or are they then to be cast off with my partner?'

"'Let not your heart be troubled,' replies the apostle, 'God reckons them to the believing, not the unbelieving parent. It is enough that they are yours. The infidelity of your partner shall never frustrate their interest in the covenant of your God. They are holy because *you* are so.'

"This decision put the subject at rest. And it lets us know that one of the reasons, if not the chief reason of the doubt, whether a married person should continue, after conversion, in the conjugal society of an infidel partner, arose from a fear lest

---

2. It is worthy of notice that this interpretation of the passage is adopted, and decisively maintained by Augustine, one of the most pious and learned divines of the fourth century. *De Sermone Domini in Monte,* ch. 27.

such continuance should exclude the children from the Church of
God. Otherwise, it is hard to comprehend why the apostle should
dissuade them from separating by such an argument as he has
employed in the text. And it is utterly inconceivable how such a
doubt could have entered their minds, had not the membership of
infants, born of believing parents, been undisputed, and esteemed
a high privilege; so high a privilege, that the apprehension of los-
ing it, made conscientious parents at a stand, whether they ought
not rather to break the ties of wedlock, by withdrawing from an
unbelieving husband or wife. Thus the origin of this difficulty, on
the one hand, and the solution of it, on the other, concur in establishing our doctrine, that, by the appointment of God Himself, the
infants of believing parents are born members of his church."[3]

10. Finally; *the history of the Christian Church, from the
apostolic age,* furnishes an argument of irresistible force in favour
of the divine authority of infant baptism.

I can assure you, my friends, with the utmost candour and
confidence, after much careful inquiry on the subject, that, for
more than fifteen hundred years after the birth of Christ, there
was not a single society of professing Christians on earth, who
opposed infant baptism on any thing like the grounds which dis-
tinguish our modern Baptist brethren. It is an *undoubted fact,* that
the people known in ecclesiastical history under the name of the
Anabaptists, who arose in Germany, in the year 1522, were the
very first body of people, in the whole Christian world, who rejected the baptism of infants, on the principles now adopted by
the Antipædobaptist body. This, I am aware, will be regarded as
an untenable position by some of the ardent friends of the Baptist
cause; but nothing can be more certain than that it is even so. Of
this a short induction of particulars will afford conclusive evidence.

Tertullian, about two hundred years after the birth of

---

3. *Essays on the Church of God*, by Dr. J.M. Mason, *Christian's Magazine,*
ii, 49, 50.

Christ, is the first man of whom we read in ecclesiastical history, as speaking a word against infant baptism; and he, while he recognizes the existence and prevalence of the practice, and expressly recommends that infants be baptized, if they are not likely to survive the period of infancy; yet advises that, where there is a prospect of their living, baptism be delayed until a late period in life. But what was the reason of this advice? The moment we look at the reason, we see that it avails nothing to the cause in support of which it is sometimes produced. Tertullian adopted the superstitious idea, that baptism was accompanied with the remission of all past sins; and that sins committed after baptism were peculiarly dangerous. He, therefore, advised, that not merely infants, but young men and young women; and even young widow and widowers should postpone their baptism until the period of youthful appetite and passion should have passed. In short, he advised that, in all cases in which death was not likely to intervene, baptism be postponed, until the subjects of it should have arrived at a period of life, when they, would be no longer in danger of being led astray by youthful lusts. And thus, for more than a century after the age of Tertullian, we find some of the most conspicuous converts to the Christian faith, postponing baptism till the close of life. Constantine the Great, we are told, though a professing Christian for many years before, was not baptized till after the commencement of his last illness. The same fact is recorded of a number of other distinguished converts to Christianity, about and after that time. But, surely, advice and facts of this kind make nothing in favour of the system of our Baptist brethren. Indeed, taken altogether, their historical bearing is strongly in favour of our system.

The next persons that we hear of as calling in question the propriety of infant baptism, were the small body of people in France, about twelve hundred years after Christ, who followed a certain Peter de Bruis, and formed an inconsiderable section of the people known in ecclesiastical history under the general name of the Waldenses. This body maintained that infants ought not to be baptized, because they were incapable of salvation. They taught

that none could be saved but those who wrought out their salvation by a long course of self-denial and labour. And as infants
were incapable of thus "working out their own salvation," they
held that making them the subjects of a sacramental seal, was an
absurdity. But surely our Baptist brethren cannot be willing to
consider these people as their predecessors, or to adopt their
creed.

We hear no more of any society or organized body of
Antipædobaptists, until the sixteenth century, when they arose, as
before stated, in Germany, and for the first time broached the
doctrine of our modern Baptist brethren. As far as I have been
able to discover, they were absolutely unknown in the whole
Christian world before that time.

But we have something more than mere negative testimony on this subject. It is not only certain, that we hear of no
society of Antipædobaptists resembling our present Baptist brethren, for more than fifteen hundred years after Christ; but we have
positive and direct proof that, during the whole of that time, infant baptism was the general and unopposed practice of the
Christian Church. To say nothing of earlier intimations, wholly
irreconcilable with any other practice than that of infant baptism,
Origen, a Greek father of the third century, and decidedly the
most learned man in his day, speaks in the most unequivocal
terms of the baptism of infants, as the general practice of the
Church in His time, and as having been received from the Apostles. His testimony is as follows: "According to the usage of the
church, baptism is given even to infants; when if there were nothing in infants which needed forgiveness and mercy, the grace of
baptism would seem to be superfluous."[4] Again; "Infants are
baptized for the forgiveness of sins. Of what sins? Or, when have
they sinned? Or, can there be any reason for the laver in their
case, unless it be according to the sense which we have mentioned above, viz: that no one is free from pollution, though he has

---

4. Homil. VIII, in Levit. ch. 12.

lived but one day upon earth? And because by baptism native pollution is taken away, therefore infants are baptized."[5] Again: "For this cause it was that the church received an order from the Apostles to give baptism even to infants."[6]

The testimony of Cyprian, a Latin Father of the third century, contemporary with Origen, is no less decisive. It is as follows:

In the year 253 after Christ, there was a Council of sixty-six bishops or pastors held at Carthage, in which Cyprian presided. To this Council, Fidus, a country pastor, presented the following question, which he wished them, by their united wisdom, to solve – viz. Whether it was necessary, in the administration of baptism, as of circumcision, to wait until the *eighth day;* or whether a child might be baptized at an earlier period after its birth? The question, it will be observed, was *not* whether infants ought to be baptized? *That* was taken for granted. But, simply, whether it was necessary to wait until the *eighth day* after their birth? The Council came *unanimously* to the following decision, and transmitted it in a letter to the inquirer.

"Cyprian and the rest of the Bishops who were present in the Council, sixty-six in number, to Fidus, our brother, greeting:

"As to the case of Infants, – whereas you judge that they must not be baptized within two or three days after they are born, and that the rule of circumcision is to be observed, that no one should be baptized and sanctified before the eighth day after he is born; we were ALL in the Council of a very different opinion. As for what you thought proper to be done, no one was of your mind; – but we all rather judged that the mercy and grace of God is to be denied to no human being that is born. This, therefore, dear brother, was our opinion in the Council; that we ought not to hinder any person from baptism, and the grace of God, who is merciful and kind to us all. And this rule, as it holds for all, we

---

5. Homil. in Luc. 14.

6. Comment. in Epist. ad Romanos. Lib. 5.

think more especially to be observed in reference to infants, even to those newly born."[7]

Surely no testimony can be more unexceptionable and decisive than this. Lord Chancellor King, in his account of the primitive Church, after quoting what is given above, and much more, subjoins the following remark: "Here, then, is a synodical decree for the baptism of infants, as formal as can possibly be expected; which being the judgment of a synod, is more authentic and cogent than that of a private father; it being supposeable that a private father might write his own particular judgment and opinion only; but the determination of a synod (and he might have added, the *unanimous* determination of a synod of sixty-six members) denotes the common practice and usage of the whole church."[8]

The famous Chrysostom, a Greek father, who flourished towards the close of the fourth century, having had occasion to speak of circumcision, and of the inconvenience and pain which attended its dispensation, proceeds to say: "But *our* circumcision, I mean the grace of *baptism,* gives cure without pain, and procures to us a thousand benefits, and fills us with the grace of the Spirit; and it has *no determinate time,* as that had; but one that is in the *very beginning of his age,* or one that is in the middle of it, or one that is in his old age, may receive this circumcision made without hands; in which there is no trouble to be undergone but to throw off the load of sins, and to receive pardon for all past offences."[9]

Passing by the testimony of several other conspicuous writers of the third and fourth centuries, in support of the fact, that infant baptism was generally practised when they wrote, I shall detain you with only one testimony more in relation to the history of this ordinance. It is that of Augustine, one of the most

---

7. Cyprian, Epist. 66.

8. *Inquiry into the Constitution,* &c. Part II. Chap. 3.

9. Homil. 40. in Genesin.

pious, learned and venerable fathers of the Christian Church, who lived a little more than three hundred years after the Apostles, – taken in connection with that of Pelagius, the learned heretic, who lived at the same time. Augustine had been pleading against Pelagius, in favor of the doctrine of original sin. In the course of this plea, he asks: "Why are infants baptized for the remission of sins, if they have no sin?" At the same time intimating to Pelagius, that if he would be consistent with himself, his denial of original sin must draw after it the denial of infant baptism. The reply of Pelagius is striking and unequivocal. "Baptism," says he, "ought to be administered to infants, with the same sacramental words which are used in the case of adult persons." – Men slander me as if I denied the sacrament of baptism to infants." – *"I never heard of any, not even the most impious heretic, who denied baptism to infants;* for who can be so impious as to hinder infants from being baptised, and born again in Christ, and so make them miss of the kingdom of God?" Again, Augustine remarks, in reference to the Pelagians: "Since they grant that infants must be baptized, as not being able to *resist the authority of the whole church, which was doubtless delivered by our Lord and His Apostles;* they must consequently grant that they stand in need of the benefit of the Mediator; that being offered by the sacrament, and by the charity of the faithful, and so being incorporated into Christ's body, they may be reconciled to God," &c. Again, speaking of certain heretics at Carthage, who, though they acknowledged infant baptism, took wrong views of its meaning, Augustine remarks: "They, *minding the Scriptures, and the authority of the whole church,* and the form of the sacrament itself, see well that baptism in infants is for the remission of sins." Further, in his work against the Donatists, the same writer speaking of baptized infants obtaining salvation without the personal exercise of faith, he says: *"which the whole body of the church holds,* as delivered to them in the case of little infants baptized; who certainly cannot believe with the heart unto righteousness, or confess with the mouth unto salvation, nay, by their crying and noise while the sacrament is administering, they disturb the holy mysteries: and

yet *no Christian man* will say that they are baptized to no purpose." Again, he says: "The custom of our mother the church in
baptizing infants must not be disregarded, nor be accounted need-
less, nor believed to be any thing else than *an ordinance delivered to us from the Apostles.*" In short, those who will be at the
trouble to consult the large extracts from the writings of Augustine, among other Christian fathers, in the learned Wall's *History
of Infant Baptism*, will find that venerable father declaring again
and again that he never met with any Christian, either of the general Church, or of any of the sects, nor with any writer, who
owned the authority of Scripture, who taught any other doctrine
than that infants were to be baptized for the remission of sin.
Here, then, were two men, undoubtedly among the most learned
then in the world – Augustine and Pelagius; the former as familiar
probably with the writings of all the distinguished fathers who had
gone before him, as any man of his time; the latter also a man of
great learning and talents, who had travelled over the greater part
of the Christian world; who both declare, about three hundred
years after the apostolic age, that they never saw or heard of any
one who called himself a Christian, not even the most impious
heretic, no nor any writer who claimed to believe in the Scriptures, who denied the baptism of infants.

Can the most incredulous reader, who is not fast bound
in the fetters of invincible prejudice, hesitate to admit, first, that
these men verily believed that infant baptism had been the universal practice of the Church from the days of the apostles; and,
secondly, that, situated and informed as they were, it was impossible that they should be mistaken?

The same Augustine, in his *Epistle to Boniface,* while he
expresses an opinion that the parents are the proper persons to
offer up their children to God in baptism, if they be good faithful
Christians; yet thinks proper to mention that others may, with
propriety, in special cases, perform the same kind office of Christian charity. "You see," says he, "that a great many are offered,
not by their parents, but by any other persons, as infant slaves are
sometimes offered by their masters. And sometimes when the par-

ents are dead, the infants are baptized, being offered by any that can afford to show this compassion on them. And sometimes infants whom their parents have cruelly exposed, may be taken up and offered in baptism by those who have no children of their own, nor design to have any." Again, in his book against the *Donatists,* speaking directly of infant baptism, he says: "If any one ask for divine authority in this matter, although that which *the whole church practises,* which *was not instituted by councils,* but was *ever in use,* is very reasonably believed to be no other than a thing delivered by the authority of the apostles; yet we may besides take a true estimate, how much the sacrament of baptism does avail infants, by the circumcision which God's ancient people received. For Abraham was justified before he received circumcision, as Cornelius was endued with the Holy Spirit before he was baptized. And yet the apostle says of Abraham, that he received the sign of circumcision, 'a seal of the righteousness of faith,' by which he had in heart believed, and it had been 'counted to him for righteousness.' Why then was he commanded to circumcise all his male infants on the eighth day, when they could not yet believe with the heart, that it might be counted to them for righteousness; but for this reason, because the sacrament is, in itself, of great importance? Therefore, as in Abraham, 'the righteousness of faith' went before, and circumcision, 'the seal of the righteousness of faith, came after;' so in Cornelius, the spiritual sanctification by the gift of the Holy Spirit went before, and the sacrament of regeneration, by the layer of baptism, came after. And as in Isaac, who was circumcised the eighth day, the seal of the righteousness of faith went before, and (as he was a follower of his father's faith) the righteousness itself, the seal whereof had gone before in his infancy, came after; so in infants baptized, the sacrament of regeneration goes before, and (if they put in practice the Christian religion) conversion of the heart, the mystery whereof went before in their body, comes after. By all which it appears, that the sacrament of baptism is one thing, and conversion of the heart another."

So much for the testimony of the Fathers. To me, I acknowledge, this testimony carries with it irresistible conviction. It is, no doubt, conceivable, considered in itself, that, in three centuries from the days of the apostles, a very material change might have taken place in regard to the subjects of baptism. But, that a change so serious and radical as that of which our Baptist brethren speak, should have been introduced without the knowledge of such men as have been just quoted, is *not conceivable.* That the Church should have passed from the practice of none but adult baptism, to that of the constant and universal baptism of infants, while such a change was utterly unknown, and never heard of, by the most active, pious, and learned men that lived during that period, cannot, I must believe, be imagined by any impartial mind. Now when Origen, Cyprian, and Chrysostom, declare, not only that the baptism of infants was the universal and unopposed practice of the Church in their respective times and places of residence; and when men of so much acquaintance with all preceding writers, and so much knowledge of all Christendom, as Augustine and Pelagius, declared that they *never heard of any one who claimed to be a Christian, either orthodox or heretic, who did not maintain and practice infant baptism;* I say, to suppose, in the face of such testimony, that the practice of infant baptism crept in, as an unwarranted innovation, between their time and that of the apostles, without the smallest notice of the change having ever reached their ears is, I must be allowed to say, of all incredible suppositions, one of the most incredible. He who can believe this, must, it appears to me, be prepared to make a sacrifice of all historical evidence at the shrine of blind and deaf prejudice.

It is here also worthy of particular notice, that those pious and far famed witnesses for the truth, commonly known by the name of the Waldenses, did undoubtedly hold the doctrine of infant baptism, and practice accordingly. In their Confessions of Faith and other writings, drawn up between the twelfth and sixteenth centuries, and in which they represent their creeds and usages as handed down, from father to son, for several hundred years before the Reformation, they speak on the subject before us so frequently and explicitly, as to preclude all doubt in regard to the fact alleged. The following specimen of their language will satisfy every reasonable inquirer.

"Baptism," say they, "is administered in a full congregation of the faithful, to the end that he that is received into the church, may be reputed and held of all as a Christian brother, and that all the congregation may pray for him, that he may be a Christian in heart, as he is outwardly esteemed to be a Christian. *And for this cause it is that we present our children in baptism,* which ought to be done by those to whom the children are most nearly related, such as their parents, or those to whom God has given this charity."

Again; referring to the superstitious additions to baptism which the Papists had introduced, they say, in one of their ecclesiastical documents: "The things which are not necessary in baptism are, the exorcisms, the breathings, the sign of the cross upon the head or forehead of the *infant,* the salt put into the mouth, the spittle into the ears and nostrils, the unction of the breast, &c. From these things many take an occasion of error and superstition, rather than of edifying and salvation."

Understanding that their Popish neighbours charged them with denying the baptism of infants, they acquit themselves of this imputation as follows:

"Neither is the time or place appointed for those who are to be baptized. But charity, and the edification of the church and congregation ought to be the rule in this matter.

"Yet, notwithstanding, *we bring our children to be baptized;* which they ought to do to whom they are most nearly related; such as their parents, or those whom God hath inspired with such a charity."

"True it is," adds the historian, "that being, for some hundreds of years, constrained to suffer their children to be baptized by the Romish priests, they deferred the performance of it as long as possible, because they detested the human inventions annexed to the institution of that holy sacrament, which they looked upon as so many pollutions of it. And by reason of their pastors, whom they called Barbes, being often abroad travelling in the service of the church, they could not have baptism administered to their children by them. They, therefore, sometimes kept them long without it. On account of which delay, the priests have charged them with that reproach. To which charge not only their adversaries have given credit, *but also many of those who have approved of their lives and faith in all other respects.* "[10]

It being so plainly a fact, established by their own unequivocal and repeated testimony, that the great body of the Waldenses were Pædobaptists, on what ground is it that our Baptist brethren assert, and that some have been found to credit the assertion, that those venerable witnesses of the truth rejected the baptism of infants? The answer is easy and ample. A small section of the people bearing the general name of Waldenses, followers of Peter de Bruis, who were mentioned in a preceding page, while they agreed with the mass of their denomination in most other matters, differed from them in regard to the subject of infant baptism. They held, as before stated, that infants were not capable of salvation; that Christian salvation is of such a nature that none can partake of it but those who undergo a course of rigorous self-denial and labour in its pursuit. Those who die in infancy not being capable of this, the Petrobrussians held that they were not capable of salvation; and, this being the case, that they ought not to be baptized. This, however, is not the doctrine of our Baptist brethren; and, of course, furnishes no support to their creed or practice. But the decisive answer is, that the Petrobrussians were a very small fraction of the great Waldensian body; probably not

---

10. See John Paul Perrin's account of the Doctrine and Order of the Waldenses and Albigenses; Sir Samuel Morland's do.; and also Leger's *Histoire Generale des Eglises Vaudoises.* Mr. William Jones, a Baptist, in a work entitled, *A History of the Waldenses,* in two volumes octavo, professes to give a full account of the Faith and Order of these pious witnesses of the truth; but, so far as I have observed, carefully leaves out of all their public formularies and other documents, every thing which would disclose their Pædobaptist principles and practice! On this artifice comment is unnecessary.

more than a thirtieth or fortieth part of the whole. The great mass of the denomination, however, as such, declare, in their Confessions of Faith, and in various public documents, that they held, and that their fathers before them, for many generations, always held, to infant baptism. The Petrobrussians, in this respect, forsook the doctrine and practice of their fathers, and departed from the proper and established Waldensian creed. If there be truth in the plainest records of ecclesiastical history, this is an undoubted fact. In short, the real state of this case may be illustrated by the following representation. Suppose it were alleged, that the Baptists in the United States are in the habit of keeping the seventh day of the week as their Sabbath? Would the statement be true? By no means. There is, indeed, a small section of the Antipædobaptist body in the United States, usually styled "Seventh day Baptists" – probably not a thirtieth part of the whole body – who observe Saturday in each week as their Sabbath. But, notwithstanding this, the proper representation, no doubt, is – (the only representation that a faithful historian of facts would pronounce correct) – that the Baptists in this country, as a general body, observe "the Lord's day" as their Sabbath. You may rest assured, my friends, that this statement most exactly illustrates the real fact with regard to the Waldenses as Pædobaptists. Twenty-nine parts, at least, out of thirty, of the whole of that body of witnesses for the truth, were undoubtedly Pædobaptists. The remaining thirtieth part departed from the faith of their fathers in regard to baptism, but departed on principles altogether unlike those of our modern Baptist brethren.

I have only one fact more to state in reference to the pious Waldenses, and that is, that soon after the opening of the Reformation by Luther, they sought intercourse with the Reformed churches of Geneva and France; held communion with them; received ministers from them; and appeared eager to testify their respect and affection for them as "brethren in the Lord." Now it is well known that the churches of Geneva and France, at this time, were in the habitual use of *infant* baptism. This single fact is sufficient to prove that the Waldenses were Pædobaptists.

If they had adopted the doctrine of our Baptist brethren, and laid the same stress on it with them, it is manifest that such intercourse would have been wholly out of the question.

If these historical statements be correct, and that they are so, is just as well attested as any facts whatever in the annals of the Church, the amount of the whole is conclusive, is *demonstrative,* that, for fifteen hundred years after Christ, the practice of infant baptism was *universal;* that to this general fact there was absolutely no exception, in the whole Christian Church, which, on principle, or even analogy, can countenance in the least degree, modern Antipædobaptism; that from the time of the apostles to the time of Luther, the general, unopposed, established practice of the Church was to regard the infant seed of believers as members of the Church, and, as such, to baptize them.

But this is not all. If the doctrine of our Baptist brethren be correct; that is, if infant baptism be a corruption and a nullity; then it follows, from the foregoing historical statements, most inevitably, that the ordinance of baptism was lost for fifteen hundred years: yes, entirely lost, from the apostolic age till the sixteenth century. For there was, manifestly, "no society, during that long period, of fifteen centuries, but what was in the habit of baptizing infants." *God had no Church, then, in the world for so long a period!* Can this be admitted? Surely not by any one who believes in the perpetuity and indestructibility of the household of faith.

Nay, if the principle of our Baptist brethren be correct, the ordinance of baptism is irrecoverably lost altogether; that is, irrecoverably without a miracle. Because if, during the long tract of time that has been mentioned, there was no true baptism in the Church; and if none but baptized persons were capable of administering true baptism to others; the consequence is plain; there is no true baptism now in the world! But can this be believed? Can we imagine that the great Head of the Church would permit one of His own precious ordinances to be banished entirely from the Church for many centuries, much less to be totally lost? Surely the thought is abhorrent to every Christian feeling.

Such is an epitome of the direct evidence in favour of infant baptism. To me, I acknowledge, it appears nothing short of *demonstration.* The invariable character of all Jehovah's dealings and covenants with the children of men; His express appointment, acted upon for two thousand years by the ancient Church; the total silence of the New Testament as to any retraction or repeal of this privilege; the evident and repeated examples of family baptism in the apostolic age; the indubitable testimony of the practice of the whole Church on the Pædobaptist plan, from the time of the apostles to the sixteenth century, including the most respectable witnesses for the truth in the dark ages; all conspire to establish on the firmest foundation, the membership, and the consequent right to baptism of the infant seed of believers. If here be no divine warrant, we may despair of finding it for any institution in the Church of God.

CHAPTER TWO

Objections Answered

"And when she was baptized, and her household, she besought us, saying – if ye have judged me to be faithful to the Lord, come into mine house, and abide there" (Acts xvi. 15).

Having adduced, in the preceding discourse, the direct evidence in support of infant baptism, let us now attend to some of the most common and popular *objections,* brought by our Baptist brethren, against the doctrine which we have attempted to establish. And,

1. The first is, that we have *no direct warrant in the New Testament, in so many words, for infant baptism.* "We are no where," say our opponents, "in the history of the apostolic age, told, in express terms, either that infants ought to be baptized, or that they were, in fact, baptized. Now is it possible to account for this omission on the supposition that such baptism was generally practised?" This objection has been urged a thousand times, with great confidence, and with no inconsiderable effect, on the minds of some serious persons of small knowledge, and of superficial thought. But when thoroughly examined, it will, I am persuaded, appear destitute of all solid foundation.

For, in the first place, even if it were as our Baptist brethren suppose; that is, even if no express warrant, in so many words, were found in the New Testament, authorizing and directing infant baptism, could this reasonably be considered, upon

Pædobaptist principles, unaccountable, or even wonderful? The
Pædobaptist principle, let it be borne in mind, is, that the Church
under the New Testament economy is the same with the Church
under the Old Testament dispensation; that the former was the
minority or childhood, the latter the maturity of the visible kingdom of the Messiah; that one of the most striking features in the
New Testament character of this kingdom is, a great increase of
light, and enlargement of privilege; that the infant seed of believers had been born in covenant with God, and their covenanted
character marked and ratified by a covenant seal, for two thousand years before Christ appeared; and that, if this privilege had
been intended simply to be continued, no new enactment was
necessary to ascertain this intention, but merely allowing it to
proceed without interposing any change. This is the ground we
take. Now, taking this ground – assuming as facts what have been
just stated as such – can any thing be more perfectly natural than
the whole aspect of the New Testament in relation to this subject?
Very little, explicit or formal, is said in reference to the covenant
standing of children, on the opening of the new economy, simply
because no material alteration as to this point was intended. All
the first Christians having been bred under the Jewish economy,
and having been always accustomed to the enjoyment of its privileges, would, of course, expect those privileges to be continued,
especially, if nothing were said about their repeal or abridgment.
To announce to these Jewish believers, that the covenant standing, and covenant advantages of their beloved children, were not
to be withdrawn or curtailed, if no other alteration in reference to
this matter, than an increase of privilege were intended, would
have been just as unnecessary as to inform them that the true God
was still to be worshipped, and the atoning sacrifice of the Messiah still regarded as the only ground of hope. In short, assuming
Pædobaptist principles, we might expect the New Testament to
exhibit precisely the aspect which it does exhibit. Not to say, in
so many words, that the privilege in question was to be continued; but all along to speak as if this were to be taken for granted,
without an explicit enactment; to assure the first Christians that

"the promise was still to them and their children;" and not to them only, but also to "as many as the Lord their God should call" into His visible Church; to tell them that, in regard to this matter, the administration of His New Testament kingdom was to be such as to abolish all distinction of sex in Christian privilege; that, in Christ, there was to be no longer a difference made between "male and female;" and, in conformity with this intimation, and as a practical comment upon it, *to introduce whole families* with the *converted parents* into the Church, by the appropriate New Testament rite, as had been invariably practised under the Old Testament economy.

But now turn, for a moment, to the opposite supposition; to that of our Baptist brethren. They are obliged, by their system, to take for granted, that, after the children of the professing people of God had been, for nearly two thousand years, in the enjoyment of an important covenant privilege – a privilege precious in itself, and peculiarly dear to the parental heart – it was suddenly, and without explanation, set aside; that on the opening of the New Testament dispensation, a dispensation of larger promises, and of increased liberality, this privilege was abruptly and totally withdrawn; that children were ejected from their former covenant relation; that they were no longer the subjects of a covenant seal, or of covenant promises; and that all this took place without one hint of any reason for it being given; without one syllable being said, in all the numerous epistles to the churches, by any one of justification or apology, for so important a change! Nay, that, instead of such notice and explanation, a mode of expression, under the new economy, should be throughout used, corresponding with the former practice, and adapted still to convey the idea that both parents and children stood in their old relation, notwithstanding the painful change! Is this credible? Can it be believed by any one who is not predetermined to regard it as true?

But if the New Testament economy does not include the church membership of the infant seed of believers, such a change, undoubtedly, did take place, on the coming in of the new economy. The Jewish disciples of Christ saw their children at once cut off from the covenant of promise, and denied its appropriate seal, to which they had always been accustomed, and in which the tenderest parental feelings were so strongly implicated. Yet we hear of no complaint on their part. We find not a word which seems intended to explain such a change, or to allay the feelings of those parents who could not fail, if such had been the fact, both to feel and to remonstrate.

I must say, my friends, that, to my mind, this consideration, if there were no other, is *conclusive*. Instead of our Baptist brethren having a right to call upon us to find a direct warrant in the New Testament, in favour of infant membership, we have a right to call upon them to produce a direct warrant for the great and sudden change which they allege took place. If it be, as they say, that the New Testament is silent on the subject, this very silence is quite sufficient to destroy their cause, and to establish ours. It affords proof positive that no such change as that which is alleged, ever occurred. That a change so important and interesting should have been introduced, without one word of explanation or apology on the part of the inspired apostles, and without one hint or struggle on the part of those who had enjoyed the former privilege; in short, that the old economy, in relation to this matter, should have been entirely broken up, and yet the whole subject passed over by the inspired writers in entire silence, is surely one of the most incredible things that can well be imagined! He who can believe it, must have a mind "fully set in him" to embrace the system which requires it.

So much on the supposition assumed by our Baptist brethren, that there is no direct warrant in the New Testament for infant membership, and of course, none for infant baptism. Admitting that the New Testament is silent on the subject, their cause is ruined. No good reason, I had almost said, no possible reason, can be assigned for such silence, in the circumstances in which the Christian Church was placed, but the fact that things, as to this point, were to go on as before. That the old privilege, so dear to the parent's heart, was to receive no other change than a *new seal,* less burdensome; applicable equally to both sexes; in a word, recognizing, extending, and perpetuating all the privileges which they had enjoyed before.

But it cannot be admitted that the New Testament contains no direct warrant for infant membership. The testimony adduced in the preceding discourse is surely worthy, to say the least, of the most serious regard. When the Master Himself declares concerning infants, "Of such is the kingdom of heaven;" when an inspired apostle proclaims: "The promise is to us and our children;" and when we plainly see, under the apostolical administration of the church, whole families received, in repeated instances, into the Church on the professed faith of the individuals who were constituted their respective heads, just as we know occurred under the old economy, when the membership of infants was undisputed; when we read such things as these in the New Testament, we surely cannot complain of the want of testimony which ought to satisfy every reasonable inquirer.

2. A second objection, often urged by our Baptist brethren, is drawn from what they insist is the *general law of positive institutions.* "In cases of moral duty," say they, "we are at liberty to argue from inference, from analogy, from implication; but in regard to positive institutions, our warrant must be direct and positive. Now, as we no where find in the New Testament any positive direction for baptizing infants, the general law, which must govern in all cases of positive institution, plainly forbids it. Here no inferential reasoning can be admitted."

This argument, I am persuaded, will not be regarded as forcible by any who examine it with attention and impartiality. The whole principle is unsound. The fact is, inferential reasoning may be, and is in many cases, quite as strong as any other. Besides, if it be contended, that in every thing relating to positive institutes, we must have direct and positive precepts, the assumed principle will prove too much.

Upon this principle, females ought never to partake of the Lord's Supper; for we have no positive precept, and no explicit example in the New Testament to warrant them in doing so, and yet our Baptist brethren, forgetting their own principle, unite with

all Christians who consider the sacramental supper as still obligatory on the Church, in admitting females to its participation. This
practice is, no doubt, perfectly right. It rests on the most solid
inferential reasoning, which may be just as strong as any other,
and which, in this case, cannot be gainsayed or resisted. But every time our Baptist brethren yield to this reasoning, and act accordingly, they desert their assumed principle.

3. A third objection frequently urged is, that if infant baptism had prevailed in the primitive Church, *we might have expected to find in the New Testament history some examples of the
children of professing Christians being baptized in their infancy.*
Our Baptist brethren remind us that the New Testament history
embraces a period of more than sixty years after the organization
of the Church, under the new economy. "Now," say they, "during
this long period, if the principle and practice of infant baptism had
been the law of the church, we must, in all probability, have found
many instances recorded of the baptism of the children of persons
already in the communion of the church. Whereas, in all that is
distinctly recorded, or occasionally hinted at, concerning the
churches of Jerusalem, Antioch, Corinth, Ephesus, Rome,
Galatia, Colosse, &c., we find no mention made of such baptisms.
We, therefore, conclude that none such occurred."

This objection, when examined, will be found, it is believed, to have quite as little weight as the preceding. The principal object of the New Testament history is to give an account of
the progress of the Gospel. Hence it was much more to the purpose of the sacred writers to inform us respecting the conversions
to Christianity from Judaism and Paganism, than to dwell in detail
on what occurred in the bosom of the Church itself. Only enough
is said on the latter subject to trace the disturbances which occurred in the churches to their proper source, and to render intel-
ligible and impressive the various precepts in relation to these
matters which are recorded for the instruction of the people of
God in all ages. Hence all the cases of baptism which are recorded, are cases in which it was administered to *converts from
Judaism, or Paganism, to Christianity.* To the best of my recol-

lection, we have no example of a single baptism of any other kind. Now this, upon Pædobaptist principles, is precisely what might have been expected. In giving a history of such churches, who would think of singling out cases of infant baptism? This is a matter so much of course, and of every day's occurrence, that it is in no respect a remarkable event, and, of course, could not be expected to be recorded as such. No wonder, then, that we find no instance of this kind specified in the annals of the apostolical Church.

But this is not all. There is connected with this fact, a still more serious difficulty, which cannot fail of bearing with most unfriendly weight on the Baptist cause. Though it is not wonderful, for the reason just mentioned, that we read of no cases of infant baptism among the Christian families of the apostolical age; yet, upon Baptist principles, it is much more difficult to be accounted for, that we find no example of persons born of Christian parents being baptized *in adult age*. Upon those principles, the children of professing Christians bear no relation to the Church. They are as completely "without" as the children of Pagans or Mohammedans, until by faith and repentance they are brought within the bond of the covenant. Their being converted and baptized, then, we might expect to be just as carefully noticed, and just as minutely detailed, as the conversion and baptism of the most complete "aliens from the commonwealth of Israel." Yet the fact is, that during the whole three score years after the ascension of Christ, which the New Testament history embraces, we have no hint of the baptism of any adult born of Christian parents. In my judgment, this fact bears very strongly in favour of the Pædobaptist cause.

4. It is objected, that *Jesus Christ Himself was not baptized until he was thirty years of age; and, therefore, it is inferred, that His disciples ought not to be baptized until they reach adult age.* To this objection I reply,

(1.) Christ was baptized by John. Now it is certain, that John's Baptism was not Christian baptism: for it is evident, from the Acts of the Apostles, that those who were baptized by John, were baptized over again, "in the name of the Lord Jesus" (chap. xix. 1-5). Besides, it is evident, from the whole passage, that the baptism of Christ by John was an essentially different thing from baptism as now practised in the Christian Church. The ministry of John the Baptist was a dispensation, if we may say so, intermediate between the Old and the New Testament economies. And, as our blessed Lord thought proper to "fulfil all righteousness," He submitted to the baptismal rite which marked that dispensation. Besides, under the Old Testament economy, when the High Priest first entered on His holy office, He was solemnly washed with water. And that officer, we know, was wont to come to the discharge of his functions at "about thirty years of age," the very age at which our Saviour was baptized, and entered on His public ministry. In like manner, when the "great High Priest of our profession," Christ Jesus, entered on His public ministry, He thought proper to comply with the same ceremony; that He might accomplish the prophecy, and fulfill all the typical representations concerning the Saviour, which had been left on record in the Old Testament Scriptures. The baptism of Christ, then, has no reference to this controversy, and cannot be made to speak either for or against our practice in regard to this ordinance. But,

(2.) If this argument have any force, it proves more than our Baptist brethren are willing to allow, viz that no person ought to be baptized under thirty years of age. So that even a real Christian, however clear his evidences of faith and repentance, though he be *twenty, twenty-five,* or even *twenty-nine* years of age, must in no case think of being baptized until he has reached the full age of thirty – a consequence so replete with absurdity, that the simple statement of it is enough to insure its refutation.

5. A fifth objection continually made by our Baptist brethren is, that *infants are not capable of those spiritual acts or exercises which the New Testament requires in order to a proper reception of the ordinance of baptism.* Thus the language of the New Testament, on various occasions, is: "Repent, and be baptized. Believe, and be baptized. If thou believest with all thine heart, thou mayest be baptized. They that gladly received the word

word were baptized. Many of the Corinthians, having believed, were baptized." In short, say our Baptist brethren, as baptism is acknowledged on all hands to be a "seal of the righteousness of faith;" and as infants are altogether incapable of exercising faith; it is, of course, not proper to baptize them.

In answer to this objection, my first remark is, that all those exhortations to faith and repentance, as prerequisites to baptism, which we find in the New Testament, are addressed to *adult persons.* And when we are called to instruct adult persons, who have never been baptized, we always address them precisely in the same way in which the apostles did. We exhort them to repent and believe, and we say, just as Philip said, "If thou believest with all thine heart, thou mayest be baptized." But this does not touch the question respecting the infant seed of believers. It only shows that when adults are baptized, such a qualification is to be urged, and such a profession required. And in this, all Pædobaptists unanimously agree.

But still, our Baptist brethren, unsatisfied with this answer, insist, that, as infants are not capable of exercising faith; as they are not capable of acting either intelligently or voluntarily in the case at all, they cannot be considered as the proper recipients of an ordinance which is represented as a "seal of the righteousness of faith." This objection is urged with unceasing confidence, and not seldom accompanied with a sneer and even ridicule, at the idea of applying a covenant seal to those who are incapable of either understanding, or giving their consent, to the transaction. It is really, my friends, enough to make one shudder to think how often, and how unceremoniously language of this kind is employed by those who acknowledge that *infants of eight days old* were once, and that by express Divine appointment, made the subjects of circumcision. Now circumcision is expressly said by the apostle to be a "seal of the righteousness of faith," as well as baptism. But were children of eight days old then capable of exercising faith, when they were circumcised, more than they are now when they are baptized? Surely the objection before us is as valid in the one case as in the other. And, whether our Baptist brethren perceive it or not, all the charges of "absurdity" and "impiety" which they are so ready to heap on infant baptism, are just as applicable to infant circumcision as to infant baptism. Are they, then, willing to say, that the application of a "seal of the righteousness of faith" to unconscious infants of eight days old, who, of course, could not exercise faith, was, under the old economy, preposterous and absurd? Are they prepared thus to "charge God foolishly"? Yet they must do it, if they would be consistent. They cannot escape from the shocking alternative. Every harsh and contemptuous epithet which they apply to infant baptism, must, if they would adhere to the principles which they lay down, be applied to infant circumcision. But that which unavoidably leads to such a consequence cannot be warranted by the Word of God.

After all, the whole weight of the objection, in this case, is founded on an entire forgetfulness of the main principle of the Pædobaptist system. It is forgotten that in every case of infant baptism, faith is required, and, if the parents be sincere, is actually exercised. But it is required of the parents, not of the children. So that, if the parent really present his child in faith, the spirit of the ordinance is entirely met and answered. It was this principle which gave meaning and legitimacy to the administration of the corresponding rite under the old dispensation. It was because the parents were visibly within the bond of the covenant, that their children were entitled to the same blessed privilege. The same principle precisely applies under the New Testament economy. Nor does it impair the force of this consideration to allege that parents, it is feared, too often present their children, in this solemn ordinance, without genuine faith. It is, indeed, probable that this is often lamentably the fact. But so it was, we cannot doubt, with respect to the corresponding ordinance, under the old dispensation. Yet the circumcision was neither invalidated, nor rendered unmeaning, by this want of sincerity on the part of the parent. It was sufficient for the visible administration that faith was visibly professed. When our Baptist brethren administer the ordinance of baptism to one who professes to repent and believe, but who is not sincere in this profession, they do not consider his want of faith as divesting the ordinance of either its warrant or its meaning. The administration may be regular and scriptural, while the recipient is criminal, and receives no spiritual benefit. It is, in every case, the profession of faith which gives the right, in the eye of the Church, to the external ordinance. The want of sincerity in this profession, while it deeply inculpates the hypocritical individual, affects not either the nature or the warrant of the administration.

6. Again; it is objected, that *baptism can do infants no good.* "Where," say our Baptist brethren, "is the *benefit* of it? What good can a little 'sprinkling with water' do a helpless, unconscious babe?" To this objection I might reply, by asking, in my turn – What good did circumcision do a Jewish child, helpless and unconscious, at eight days old? To ask the question is almost impious, because it implies an impeachment of infinite wisdom.[1] God appointed that ordinance to be administered to infants. And, accordingly, when the apostle asked, in the spirit of some modern cavillers, "What profit is there of circumcision?" He replies, *"much, every way."* In like manner, when it is asked, "What profit is there in baptising our infant children?" I answer, *Much, every way.* Baptism is a sign of many important truths, and a seal of many important covenant blessings. Is there no advantage in attending on an ordinance which holds up to our view, in the most impressive symbolical language, several of those fundamental doctrines of the Gospel which are of the deepest interest to us and our offspring; such as our fallen, guilty, and polluted state by nature, and the method appointed by infinite wisdom and love for our recovery, by the atoning blood, and cleansing Spirit of the Saviour? Is there no advantage in solemnly dedicating our children to God, by an appropriate rite, of His own appointment? Is there no advantage in formally binding ourselves, by covenant en-

---

1. A grave and respectable Baptist minister, in the course of an argument on this subject, candidly acknowledged that the administration of circumcision to an infant eight days old, would have appeared to him a useless, and even a silly rite! An honest, and certainly a very natural confession!

gagements, to bring up our offspring "in the nurture and admonition of the Lord"? Is there no advantage in publicly ratifying the connection of our children, as well as ourselves, with the visible Church, and, as it were, binding them to an alliance with the God of their fathers? Is there nothing, either comforting or useful in solemnly recognising as our own that covenant promise, "I will establish my covenant between me and thee, and *thy seed after thee, to be a God to thee and thy seed after thee"?* Is it a step of no value to our children themselves, to be brought, by a divinely appointed ordinance, into the bosom, and to the notice, the maternal attentions, and the prayers of the Church, "the mother of us all"? And is it of no advantage to the parents, in educating their children, to be able to remind them, from time to time, that they have been symbolically sanctified, or set apart, by the seal of Jehovah's covenant, and to plead with them by the solemn vows which they have made on their behalf? Verily, my dear friends, those who refuse or neglect the baptism of their children, not only sin against Christ, by disobeying His solemn command; but they also deprive both themselves and their children of great benefits. They may imagine that, as it is a disputed point, it may be a matter of indifference, whether their children receive this ordinance in their infancy, or grow up unbaptized. But is not this attempting to be wiser than God? I do not profess to know all the advantages attendant or consequent on the administration of this significant and divinely appointed rite; but one thing I know, and that is, that Christ has appointed it as a sign of precious truths, and a seal of rich blessings, to His covenant people, and their infant offspring; and I have no doubt that, in a multitude of cases, the baptized children, presented by professing parents who had no true faith, but who, by this act, brought their children within the care, the watch, and the privileges of the Church, have been instrumental in conferring upon their offspring rich benefits, while they themselves went down to everlasting burnings. If I mistake not, I have seen many cases, in which, as far as the eye of man could go, the truth of this remark has been signally exemplified.

Let it not be said, that such a solemn dedication of a child to God, is usurping the rights of the child to judge and act for himself, when he comes to years of discretion; and that it is inconsistent with the privilege of every rational being to free inquiry, and free agency. This objection is founded on an infidel spirit. It is equally opposed to the religious education of children; and, if followed out, would militate against all those restraints, and that instruction which the Word of God enjoins on parents. Nay, if the principle of this objection be correct, it is wrong to pre-occupy the minds of our children with an abhorrence of lying, theft, drunkenness, malice, and murder; lest, forsooth, we should fill them with such prejudices as would be unfriendly to free inquiry.

The truth is, one great purpose for which the Church was instituted, is to watch over and train up children in the knowledge and fear of God, and thus, to "prepare a seed to serve him, who should be accounted to the Lord for a generation." And I will venture to say, that that system of religion which does not embrace children in its ecclesiastical provisions, and in its covenant engagements, is most materially defective. Infants may not receive any apparent benefit from baptism, at the moment in which the ordinance is administered; although a gracious God may, even then, accompany the outward emblem with the blessing which it represents, even "the washing of regeneration, and the renewing of the Holy Spirit." This, indeed, may not be, and most commonly, so far as we can judge, is not the case. But still the benefits of this ordinance, when faithfully applied by ministers, and faithfully received by parents, are abundant – nay, great and important every way. When children are baptized, they are thereby recognized as belonging to the visible Church of God. They are, as it were, solemnly entered as scholars or disciples in the school of Christ. They are brought into a situation, in which they not only may be trained up for God, but in which their parents are *bound* so to train them up; and the church is bound to see that they be so trained, as that the Lord's claim to them shall ever be recognized and maintained. In a word, by baptism, when the administrators and recipients are both faithful to their respective trusts, children are brought into a situation in which all the means of grace; all the privileges pertaining to Christ's covenanted family; in a word, all that is comprehended under the broad and precious import of the term *Christian education,* is secured to them in the most ample manner. Let parents think of this, when they come to present their children in this holy ordinance. And let children lay all this to heart, when they come to years in which they are capable of remembering and realizing their solemn responsibility.

7. A seventh objection which our Baptist brethren frequently urge is, that, upon our plan, *the result of baptism seldom corresponds with its professed meaning. We say it is a symbol of regeneration; but experience proves that a great majority of those infants who are baptized never partake of the grace of regeneration.* The practice of Pædobaptists, they tell us, is adapted to corrupt the Church to the most extreme degree, by filling it with unconverted persons. To this objection we reply:

That baptism is not more generally connected or followed with that spiritual benefit of which it is a striking emblem, is indeed to be lamented. But still this acknowledged fact does not, it is believed, either destroy the significance of the ordinance, or prove it to be useless. If it hold up to view, to all who behold it, every time that it is administered, the nature and necessity of regeneration by the Holy Spirit; if it enjoin, and, to a very desirable extent, secure, to the children of the church enlightened and faithful instruction, in the great doctrines of the Gospel, and this doctrine of spiritual cleansing in particular; and if it is, in a multitude of cases, actually connected with precious privileges, and saving benefits; we have, surely, no right to conclude that it is of small advantage, because it is not in all cases followed by the blessing which it symbolically represents. How many read the Bible without profit! How many attend upon the external service of prayer, without sincerity, and without a saving blessing! But are the reading of the Scriptures, and the duty of prayer less obligatory, or of more dubious value on that account? In truth, the same objection might be made to circumcision. That, as well as baptism, was a symbol of regeneration, and of spiritual cleansing: but how many received the outward symbol without the spiritual benefit? The fact is, the same objection may be brought against every institution of God. They are all richly significant, and abound in spiritual meaning, and in spiritual instruction; but their influence is moral, and may be defeated by unbelief. They cannot exert a physical power, or convert and save by their inherent energy. Hence they are often attended by many individuals, without benefit; but still their administration is by no means, in respect to the Church of God, in vain in the Lord. It is daily exerting an influence of which no human arithmetic can form an accurate estimate. Thousands, no doubt, even of baptized *adults* receive the ordinance without faith, and, of course, without saving profit. But thousands more receive it in faith, and in connexion with those precious benefits of which it is a symbol. This is the case with all ordinances; but because they are not always connected with saving benefits, we are neither to disparage, nor cease to recommend them.

But if baptism be a symbol of regeneration; if it hold forth to all who receive it, either for themselves or their offspring, the importance and necessity of this great work of God's grace; if it bind them to teach their children, as soon as they become capable of receiving instruction, this vital truth, as well as all the other fundamental truths of our holy religion; if, in consequence of their baptism, children are recognized as bearing a most important relation to the Church of God, as bound by her rules, and responsible to her tribunal; and if all these principles be faithfully carried out into practice; can our children be placed in circumstances more favourable to their moral benefit? If not regenerated at the time of baptism (which the nature of the ordinance does not necessarily imply), are they not, in virtue of their connexion with the church, thus ratified and sealed, placed in the best of all schools for learning, practically, as well as doctrinally, the things of God? Are they not, by these means, even when they fail of becoming pious, restrained and regulated, and made better members of society? And are not multitudes of them, after all, brought back from their temporary wanderings, and by the reviving influence of their baptismal seal, and their early training, made wise unto salvation? Let none say, then, that infant baptism seldom realizes its symbolical meaning. It is, I apprehend, made to do this far more frequently than is commonly imagined. And if those who offer them up to God in this ordinance, were more faithful, this favourable result would occur with a frequency more than ten-fold.

8. A further objection often urged by the opponents of infant baptism is, that *we have the same historical evidence for infant communion that we have infant baptism*; and that the evidence of the former in the early history of the Church, altogether invalidates the historical testimony which we find in favour of the latter.

In reply to this objection, it is freely granted, that the practice of administering the eucharist to children, and sometimes even to very young children, infants, has been in use in various parts of the Christian Church from an early period, and is, in some parts of the nominally Christian world, still maintained. About the middle of the third century, we hear of it in some of the African churches. A misconception of the Saviour's words: "Except ye eat the flesh of the Son of man, and drink his blood, ye have no life in you" – led many to believe that a participation of the Lord's supper was essential to salvation. They were, therefore, led to give a small portion of the sacramental bread dipped in wine to children, and dying persons, who were not able to receive it in the usual form; and, in some cases, we find that this morsel of bread moistened with the consecrated wine was even forced down the throats of infants, who were reluctant or unable to swallow it. Nay, to so revolting a length was this superstition carried in a few churches, that the consecrated bread and wine united in the same manner as in the case of infants, were thrust into the mouths of the *dead,* who had departed without receiving them during life!

But it is doing great injustice to the cause of infant baptism to represent it as resting on no better ground than the practice of infant communion. The following points of difference are manifest, and appear to me perfectly conclusive.

(1.) Infant communion derives not the smallest countenance from the Word of God; whereas, with regard to infant baptism, we find in Scripture its most solid and decisive support. It would rest on a firm foundation if every testimony out of the Bible were destroyed.

(2.) The historical testimony in favour of infant communion, is greatly inferior to that which we possess in favour of infant baptism. We have no hint of the former having been in use in any church until the time of Cyprian, about the middle of the third century; whereas testimony more or less clear in favour of the latter has come down to us from the apostolic age.

(3.) Once more: Infant communion by no means stands on a level with infant baptism as to its *universal* or even *general* reception. We find two eminent men in the fourth century, among the most learned then on earth, and who had enjoyed the best opportunity of becoming acquainted with the whole Church, declaring that the baptism of infants was a practice which had come down from the apostles, and was universally practised in the Church; nay, that they had never heard of any professing Christians in the world, either orthodox or heretical, who did not baptize their children. But we have no testimony approaching this, in proof of the early and universal adoption of infant communion. It was manifestly an innovation, founded on principles which, though, to a melancholy degree prevalent, were never universally received. And as miserable superstition brought it into the Church, so a still more miserable superstition destroyed it. When transubstantiation arose, the sacred elements (now transmuted, as was supposed, into the real body and blood of the Saviour) began to be considered as too awful in their character to be imparted to children. But in the Greek Church, who separated from the Latin before transubstantiation was established, the practice of infant communion still superstitiously continues.

9. Again: It is objected that *Pædobaptists are not consistent with themselves, in that they do not treat their children as if*

they were members of the Church. "Pædobaptists," say our Baptist brethren, "maintain that the children of professing Christians are, in virtue of their birth, members of the church – plenary members – externally in covenant with God, and as such made the subjects of a sacramental seal. Yet we seldom or never see a Pædobaptist church *treating her baptized children as church members,* that is, instructing, watching over, and disciplining them, as in the case of adult members. Does not this manifest that their system is inconsistent with itself, impracticable, and therefore unsound?" This objection is a most serious and weighty one, and ought to engage the conscientious attention of every Pædobaptist who wishes to maintain his profession with consistency and to edification.

It cannot be denied, then, that the great mass of the Pædobaptist churches do act inconsistently in regard to this matter. They do not carry out, and apply their own system by a corresponding practice. That baptized children should be treated by the church and her officers just as other children are treated: that they should receive the seal of a covenant relation to God and His people, and then be left to negligence and sin, without official inspection, and without discipline, precisely as those are left who bear no relation to the church, is, it must be confessed, altogether inconsistent with the nature and design of the ordinance, and in a high degree unfriendly to the best interests of the Church of God. This distressing fact, however, as has been often observed, militates, not against the doctrine itself, of infant membership, but against the inconsistency of those who profess to adopt and to act upon it.

If one great end of instituting a church, as was before observed, is the training up of a godly seed in the way of truth, holiness, and salvation; and if one great purpose of sacramental seals is to "separate between the precious and the vile," and to set a distinguishing mark upon the Lord's people; then, undoubtedly, those who bear this mark, whether infant or adult, ought to be treated with appropriate inspection and care, and their relation to the Church of God never, for a moment, lost sight of or neglected.

In regard to adults, this duty is generally recognized by all evangelical churches. Why it has fallen into so much neglect, in regard to our infant and juvenile members, may be more easily explained than justified. And yet it is manifest, that attention to the duty in question in reference to the youthful members of the church, is not only important, but, in some respects, pre-eminently so; and peculiarly adapted to promote the edification and enlargement of the Christian family.

If it be asked, what more can be done for the moral culture and welfare of baptized children, than is done? I answer, *much,* that would be of inestimable value to them, and to the Christian community. The task, indeed, of training them up for God, is an arduous one, but it is practicable, and the faithful discharge of it involves the richest reward. The following plan may be said naturally to grow out of the doctrine of infant membership; and no one can doubt that, if carried into faithful execution, it would form a new and glorious era in the history of the Church of God.

Let all baptized children, from the hour of their receiving the seal of God's covenant, be recorded and recognized as infant disciples. Let the officers of the church, as well as their parents according to the flesh, ever regard them with a watchful and affectionate eye. Let Christian instruction, Christian restraint, and Christian warning, entreaty and prayer ever attend them, from the mother's lap to the infant school, and from the infant school to the seminary, whatever it may be, for more mature instruction. Let them be early taught to reverence and read the Word of God, and to treasure up select portions of it in their memories. Let appropriate catechisms, and other sound compends of Christian truth, be put into their hands, and by incessant repetition and inculcation be impressed upon their minds. Let a school, or schools, according to its extent, be established in each church, placed under the immediate instruction of exemplary, orthodox, and pious teachers, carefully superintended by the pastor, and visited as often as practicable by all the officers of the church. Let these beloved youth be often reminded of the relation which they bear to the Christian family; and the just claim of Christ to their affections and service be often presented with distinctness, solemnity, and affection. Let every kind of error and immorality be faithfully reproved, and, as far as possible, suppressed in them. Let the pastor convene the baptized children as often as practicable, and address them with instruction and exhortation in the name of that God to whom they have been dedicated, and every endeavour made to impress their consciences and their hearts with Gospel truth. When they come to years of discretion, let them be affectionately reminded of their duty to ratify, by their own act, the vows made by their parents in baptism, and be urged, again and again, to give, first their hearts, and then the humble acknowledgment of an outward profession, to the Saviour. Let this plan be pursued faithfully, constantly, patiently, and with parental tenderness. If instruction and exhortation be disregarded, and a course of error, immorality, or negligence be indulged in, let warning, admonition, suspension, or excommunication ensue, according to the character of the individual, and the exigencies of the case. "What!" some will be disposed to say, "suspend or excommunicate a young person, who has never yet taken his seat at a sacramental table, nor even asked for that privilege?" Certainly. Why not? If the children of professing Christians are born members of the church, and are baptized as a sign and seal of this membership, nothing can be plainer than that they ought to be treated in every respect as church members, and, of course, if they act in an unchristian manner, a bar ought to be set up in the way of their enjoying Christian privileges. If this be not admitted, we must give up the very first principles of ecclesiastical order and duty. Nor is there, obviously, any thing more incongruous in suspending or excluding from church privileges a young man, or young woman, who has been baptized in infancy, and trained up in the bosom of the church, but has now no regard for religion, than there is in suspending or excommunicating one who has been, for many years, an attendant on the Lord's table, but has now forsaken the house of God, and has no longer any desire to approach a Christian ordinance. No one would consider it as

either incongruous or unreasonable to declare such a person unworthy of Christian fellowship, and excluded from it, though he
had no disposition to enjoy it. The very same principle applies in
the case now under consideration.

It has been supposed, indeed, by some Pædobaptists, that
although every baptized child is a regular church member, he is
a member only of the general visible Church, and not in the ordinary sense, of any particular church; and, therefore, that he is not
amenable to ecclesiastical discipline until he formally connects
himself with some particular church. This doctrine appears to me
subversive of every principle of ecclesiastical order. Every baptized child is, undoubtedly, to be considered as a member of the
church in which he received baptism, until he dies, is excommuni-
cated, or regularly dismissed to another church. And if the time
shall ever come when all our churches shall act upon this plan;
when infant members shall be watched over with unceasing and
affectionate moral care; when a baptized young person, of either
sex, being not yet what is called a communicant, shall be made
the subject of mild but faithful Christian discipline, if he fall into
heresy or immorality; when he shall be regularly dismissed, by
letter, from the watch and care of one church to another; and
when all his spiritual interests shall be guarded by the church, as
well as by his parents, with sacred and affectionate diligence;
when this efficient and faithful system shall be acted upon, infant
baptism will be universally acknowledged as a blessing, and the
Church will shine with new and spiritual glory.

The truth is, if infant baptism were properly improved; if
the profession which it includes, and the obligations which it imposes, were suitably appreciated and followed up, it would have
few opponents. I can no more doubt, if this were done, that it
would be blessed to the saving conversion of thousands of our
young people, than I can doubt the faithfulness of a covenant
God. Yes, infant baptism is of God, but the fault lies in the conduct of its advocates. The inconsistency of its friends, has done
more to discredit it, than all the arguments of its opposers, a hundred fold. Let us hope that these friends will, one day, arouse from

their deplorable lethargy, and show that they are contending for
an ordinance as precious as it is scriptural.

10. Another objection, often urged with confidence,
against infant membership and baptism, is, that, *if they be well
founded, then it follows, of course, that every baptized young
person, or even child, who feels disposed to do so, has a right to
come to the Lord's table, without inquiry or permission of any
one.* Upon this principle, say our Baptist brethren, as a large portion of those who are baptized in infancy are manifestly not pious,
and many of them become openly profligate; if their caprice or
their wickedness should prompt them to go forward, the church
would be disgraced by crowds of the most unworthy communicants.

This objection is founded on an entire mistake. And a
recurrence, for one moment, to the principles of civil society, will
at once expose it. Every child is a citizen of the country in which
he was born; a plenary citizen: there is no such thing as half-way
citizenship in this case. He is a free born citizen in the fullest extent of the term. Yet, until he reach a certain age, and possess
certain qualifications, he is not eligible to the most important
offices which his country has to confer. And after he has been
elected, he cannot take his seat for the discharge of these official
functions, until he has taken certain prescribed oaths. It is evident
that the State has a right, and finds it essential to her well being,
by her constitution and her laws, thus to limit the rights of the
citizen. Still no one supposes that he is the less a citizen, or thinks
of representing him as only a half-way citizen prior to his compli-
ance with these forms. In like manner every baptized child is a
member – a plenary member of the church in which he received
the sacramental seal. There his membership is recognized and
recorded, and there alone can he regularly receive a certificate of
this fact, and a dismission to put himself under the watch and care
of any other church. Still the church to which this ecclesiastical
minor belongs, in the exercise of that "authority which Christ has
given, for edification and not for destruction," will not suffer him,
if she does her duty, to come to the Lord's table, until he has

reached an age when he has "knowledge to discern the Lord's body," and until he shall manifest that exemplary deportment and hopeful piety which become one who claims the privileges of Christian communion. If he manifest an opposite character, it is her duty, as a part of her stated discipline, to prevent his enjoying these privileges; just as it is her duty, in the case of one who has been a communicant for years, when he departs from the order and purity of a Christian profession, to debar him from the continued enjoyment of his former good standing. In short, the language of the apostle Paul, though originally intended for a different purpose, is strictly applicable to the subject before us: "The heir, as long as he is a child, differeth nothing from a servant, though he be lord of all; but is under tutors and governors, until the time appointed of the Father." In a word, in the Church, as well as in the State, there is an order in which privileges are to be enjoyed. As it is not every citizen who is eligible to office; and as not even the qualified have a right to intrude into office uncalled; so youthful church members, like all others, are under the watch and care of the church, and the time and manner in which they shall recognize their baptismal engagements, and come to the enjoyment of plenary privileges, Christ has left His Church to decide, on her responsibility to Himself. No one, of any age, has a right to come to her communion without the consent of the Church. When one, after coming to that communion, has been debarred from it for a time, by regular ecclesiastical authority, he has no right to come again until the interdict is taken off. Of course, by parity of reasoning, one who has never yet come at all, cannot come without asking and obtaining the permission of those who are set to govern in the Church.

This view of the subject is at once illustrated and confirmed by the uniform practice of the Old Testament Church. The children of Jewish parents, though regular church members in virtue of their birth, and recognized as such in virtue of their circumcision, were still not allowed to come to the Passover until they were of a certain age, and not even then, unless they were ceremonially clean. This is so well attested by sacred antiquarians, both Jewish and Christian, that it cannot be reasonably called in question. Calvin remarks, that "the Passover, which has now been succeeded by the sacred Supper, did not admit guests of all descriptions promiscuously; but was rightly eaten only by those who were of sufficient age to be able to inquire into its signification." The same distinct statement is also made by the Rev. Dr. Gill, an eminent commentator of the Baptist denomination. "According to the maxims of the Jews," says he, "persons were not obliged to the duties of the law, or subject to the penalties of it in case of non-performance, until they were, a female, at the age of twelve years and one day, and a male at the age of thirteen years and one day. But then they used to train up their children, and inure them to religious exercises before. They were not properly under the law until they were arrived at the age abovementioned; nor were they reckoned *adult* church members until then; nor then neither unless worthy persons: for so it is said, 'He that is worthy, at thirteen years of age, is called' a 'son of the congregation of Israel.'"[2]

The objection, then, before us is of no force. Or rather, the fact which it alleges and deprecates has no existence. It makes no part of the Pædobaptist system. Nay, our system has advantages in respect to this matter – great and radical advantages, which belong to no other. While it regards baptized children as members of the church, and solemnly binds the church, as well as the parents, to see that they be faithfully trained up "in the nurture and admonition of the Lord," it recognizes the church as possessing, and as bound to exercise, the power of guarding her communion table from all the profane approaches, even of her own children, and so regulating their Christian culture, and their personal recognition of Christian duty, as shall best serve the great purpose of building up the Church as "an habitation of God through the Spirit."

11. The last objection which I propose to consider is this:

---

2. Commentary on Luke ii. 42.

"If baptism," say our opponents, "takes the place of circumcision, and if the church is the same in substance now as when circumcision was the initiating seal, then *why is not baptism as universal in the New Testament church, as circumcision was under the old economy?* Why is not every child, under the light of the Gospel, baptized, as every Israelitish child was circumcised?" I answer, this, undoubtedly, *ought to be the case.* That is, all parents, where the Gospel comes, ought to be true believers; ought to be members of the Church of Christ themselves; and ought to dedicate their children to God in holy baptism. The command of God calls for it; and if parents were what they ought to be, they would be all prepared for a proper application of this sacramental seal. Under the Mosaic dispensation, a single nation of the great human family, was called out of an idolatrous world to be the depository of the word and the ordinances of the true God. Then all who belonged to that nation were bound to be holy; and unless they were at least ceremonially clean, the divine direction was, that they should be "cut off from their people." The obligation was universal, and the penalty, in case of delinquency, was universal. Multitudes of parents, no doubt, under that economy, presented their children to God in the sacrament of circumcision, who had no true faith; 'but they professed to believe; they attended to all the requisitions of ceremonial cleanness, and that rendered the circumcision authorized and regular. So in the New Testament Church. This is a body, like the other, called out from the rest of mankind, but not confined to a particular nation. It consists of all those, of every nation, who profess the true religion. Within this spiritual community, baptism ought to be as universal as circumcision was in the old "commonwealth of Israel." Those parents who profess faith in Christ, and obedience to Him, and those only, ought to present their children in baptism. There is, indeed, reason to fear that many visible adult members are not sincere. Still, as they are externally regular, their children are entitled to baptism. And were the whole infant population of our land in these circumstances, they might, and ought to be baptized.

I have thus endeavoured to dispose of the various objections which our Baptist brethren are wont to urge against the cause of infant baptism. I have conscientiously aimed to present them in all their force; and am constrained to believe that neither Scripture, reason, nor ecclesiastical history afford them the least countenance. The longer I reflect on the subject, the deeper is my conviction, that the membership and the baptism of infants rest on grounds which no fair argument can shake or weaken.

From the principles implied or established in the foregoing pages, we may deduce the following practical conclusions:

1. We are warranted in returning with renewed confidence to the conclusion stated in advance, in the early part of our first discourse, viz: that the error of our Baptist brethren in rejecting the church membership and the baptism of infants, *is a most serious and mischievous error.* It is not a mere mistake about a speculative point; but is an error which so directly contravenes the spirit of the whole Bible, and of all Jehovah's covenants with His people, in every age, that it must be considered as invading some of the most vital interests of the body of Christ, and as adapted to exert a most baneful influence on His spiritual kingdom. On this subject, my friends, my expressions are strong, because my convictions are strong, and my desire to guard every hearer against mischievous error increasingly strong. I am, indeed, by no means disposed to deny either the piety or the honest convictions of our respected Baptist brethren in adopting an opposite opinion from ours. But I am, nevertheless, deeply convinced that their system is not only entirely unscriptural, but also that its native tendency is to place children, who are the hope of the Church, in a situation less friendly to the welfare of Zion, and less favourable, by far, to their own salvation, than that in which they are placed by our system; and that its ultimate influence on the rising generation, on family religion, and on the growth of the Church, must be deeply injurious.

2. Again; it is evident, from what has been said, that *the baptism of our children means much, and involves much solemn tender obligation.* We do not, indeed, ascribe to this sacrament

that kind of inherent virtue of which some who bear the Christian name have spoken and inferred so much. We do not believe that baptism is regeneration.[3] We consider this as a doctrine having no foundation in the Word of God, and as eminently fitted to deceive and destroy the soul. We do not suppose that the ordinance, whenever legitimately administered, is necessarily accompanied with any physical or moral influence, operating either on the soul or the body of him who receives it. Yet, on the other hand, we do not consider it as a mere unmeaning ceremony. We cannot regard it as the mere giving a name to the child to whom it is dispensed. Multitudes appear to regard it as amounting to little, if any more than one or both of these. And, therefore, they consider the season of its celebration as a kind of ecclesiastical festival or pageant. They would not, on any account, have the baptism of their children neglected; and yet they solicit and receive it for their offspring with scarcely one serious or appropriate thought; without any enlightened or adequate impression of what it means, or what obligation it imposes on them or their children. A baptism, like a marriage, is regarded by multitudes as an appropriate season for congratulation and feasting, and very little more, in connexion with it, seems to occur to their minds. This is deeply to be deplored. The minds of the mass of mankind seem to be ever prone to vibrate from superstition to impiety, and from impiety back to superstition. Those simple, spiritual views of truth, and of Christian ordinances which the Bible every where holds forth, and which alone tend to real benefit, too seldom enlighten and govern the mass of those who bear the Christian name. Now, the truth is, little as it is recollected and laid to heart, few things can be more expressive, more solemn, or more interesting, more touching in its appeals, more deeply comprehensive in its import, or more weighty in the obligations which it involves, than the baptism of an infant. I repeat it – and oh, that the sentence could be made to thrill through every parent's heart in

_____

3. See Appendix Two.

Christendom – the baptism of a child is one of the solemn transactions pertaining to our holy religion. A human being, just opening its eyes on the world; presented to that God who made it; devoted to that Saviour without an interest in whose atoning blood, it had better never have been born; and consecrated to that Holy Spirit, who alone can sanctify and prepare it for heaven; is indeed a spectacle adapted to affect every pious heart. In death, our race is run; worldly hope and expectation are alike extinct; and the destiny of the immortal spirit is forever fixed. But the child presented for baptism, if it reach the ordinary limit of human life, has before it many a trial; and will need all the pardoning mercy, all the sanctifying grace, and all the precious consolations which the blessed Gospel of Christ has to bestow. And even if it die in infancy, it still needs the pardoning mercy and sanctifying grace which are set forth in this ordinance. On either supposition, the transaction is important. A course is commenced which will be a blessing or a curse beyond the power of the human mind to estimate. And the eternal happiness or misery of the young immortal will depend, under God, upon the training it shall receive from the hands of those who offer it.

Let those, then, who bring their children to the sacred font to be baptized, ponder well what this ordinance means, and what its reception involves, both in regard to parents and children. Let them remember that in taking this step, we make a solemn profession of belief, that our children, as well as ourselves, are born in sin, and stand in indispensable need of pardoning mercy and sanctifying grace. We formally dedicate them to God, that they may be "washed and justified, and sanctified in the name of the Lord Jesus, and by the Spirit of our God." And we take upon ourselves solemn vows to train them up in the knowledge and fear of God; to instruct them, from the earliest dawn of reason, in the principles and duties of our holy religion; to consider and treat them as ingrafted members of the family of Christ; and to do all in our power, by precept and example, by authority and by prayer, to lead them in the ways of truth, of holiness, and of salvation. Is this an ordinance to be engaged in as a mere ceremony, or with convivial levity? Surely if there be a transaction, among all the duties incumbent on us as Christians – if there be a transaction which ought to be engaged in with reverence, and godly fear; with penitence, faith, and love; with bowels of Christian compassion yearning over our beloved offspring; with humble and importunate aspirations to the God of all grace for His blessing on them and ourselves; and with solemn resolutions, in the strength of His grace, that we will be faithful to our vows, – this is that transaction! O how full of meaning! And yet how little thought of by the most of those who engage in it with external decorum!

3. The foregoing discussion will show *by whom children ought to be presented in holy baptism.* The answer given by the old Waldenses to this question is, undoubtedly, the wisest and best. They say, as before quoted, "Children ought to be presented in baptism by those to whom they are most nearly related, such as their parents, or those whom God hath inspired with such a charity." If parents be living, and be of a suitable character – that is, if they have been baptized themselves, and sustain a regular standing as professing Christians – they, and they alone, ought to present their children in this ordinance. And all introduction of godfathers and godmothers, as sponsors, either instead of the parents, or besides the parents, is regarded by the great majority of Pædobaptist churches as superstitious, unwarranted, and, of course, mischievous in its tendency. Whatever tends to beget erroneous ideas of the nature and design of a Gospel ordinance; to shift off the responsibility attending it from the proper to improper hands; and to the assumption of solemn engagements by those who can never really fulfill them, and have no intention of doing it, cannot fail of exerting an influence unfriendly to the best interests of the Church of God.

But if the parents be dead; or, though living, of irreligious character; and if the grand-parents, or any other near relations, of suitable qualifications, be willing to undertake the office of training up children "in the nurture and admonition of the Lord," it is proper for them to present such children in baptism. Or if deserted, or orphan children be cast in the families of strangers, who are no way related to them according to the flesh, but who are willing to stand in the place of parents, and train them up for God; even these strangers, in short, any and every person, of suitable character, who may be willing to assume the charitable office of giving them a Christian education, may and ought to present such children for Christian baptism. Not only the offspring of Abraham's body, but "all that were born in his house, and all that were bought with his money," were commanded to be circumcised. Surely no Christian, who has a child, white or black, placed in his family, and likely to be a permanent member of it, can doubt that it is his duty to give it a faithful Christian education. And as one great object of infant baptism is to secure this point, he will not hesitate to offer it up to God in that ordinance which He has appointed, provided no valid objection in regard to the wishes of the parents of such a child interpose to prevent it.

4. This subject shows *how responsible, and how solemn is the situation of those young persons who have been in their infancy dedicated to God in holy baptism!* This is a point concerning which both old and young are too often forgetful. It is generally conceded, and extensively felt, that parents, by dedicating their children to God in this ordinance, are brought under very weighty obligations, which cannot be forgotten by them, without incurring great guilt. But young people seldom lay to heart as they ought, that their early reception of the seal of God's covenant, in consequence of the act of their parents, places them in circumstances of the most solemn and responsible kind. They are too apt to imagine that they are not members of the church, until by some act of profession of their own, they are brought into this relation, and assume its bonds; that their making this profession, or not making it is a matter of mere choice, left to their own decision; that by omitting it, they violate no tie – contract no guilt; that by refraining, they leave themselves more at liberty; and that the only danger consists in making an insincere profession. This is a view of the subject, which, however common, is totally, and most criminally erroneous. The children of professing Christians are already in the church. They were born members. Their bap-

tism did not make them members. It was a public ratification and recognition of their membership. They were baptized because they were members. They received the seal of the covenant because they were already in covenant by virtue of their birth. This blessed privilege is their "birth-right." Of course, the only question they can ask themselves is, not – shall we enter the church, and profess to be connected with Christ's family? But – shall we continue in it, or act the part of ungrateful deserters? Shall we be thankful for this privilege, and gratefully recognize and confirm it by our own act; or shall we renounce our baptism; disown and deny the Saviour in whose name we have been enrolled as members of His family; and become open apostates from that family? This is the real question to be decided; and truly a solemn question it is! Baptized young people! think of this. You have been in the bosom of the Church ever since you drew your first breath. The seal of God's covenant has been placed upon you. You cannot, if you would, escape from the responsibility of this relation. You may forget it; you may hate to think of it; you may despise it; but still the obligation lies upon you; you cannot throw it off. Your situation is solemn beyond expression. On the one hand, to go forward, and to recognize your obligation by a personal profession, without any love to the Saviour, is to insult Him by a heartless offering; and, on the other, to renounce your allegiance by refusing to acknowledge Him, by turning your backs on His ordinances, and by indulging in that course of life by which His religion is dishonoured, is certainly, whether you realize it or not, to "deny him before men," and to incur the fearful guilt of apostacy; of "drawing back unto perdition."

"According to this representation," I shall be told, "the condition of many of our youth is very deplorable. It is their duty, you say, to profess the name of Christ, and to seal their profession at a sacramental table. This they cannot do; for they are conscious that they do not possess those principles and dispositions which are requisite to render such a profession honest. What course shall they steer? If they do not profess Christ, they live in rebellion against God: if they do, they mock Him with a lie. Which side of the alternative shall they embrace? Continue among the profane, and be consistently wicked? Or withdraw from them in appearance, and play the hypocrite?"

The case is, indeed, very deplorable. Destruction is on either hand. For "the *unbelieving* shall have their part in the lake of fire" (Rev. xxi. 6); and "the hope of the *hypocrite* shall perish" (Job viii. 13). God forbid that we should encourage either a false profession, or a refusal to make one. The duty is to embrace neither side of the alternative. Not to continue with the profane, and not to act the hypocrite; but to receive the Lord Jesus Christ in truth, and to walk in Him. "I *cannot* do it," replies one: and one, it may be, not without moments of serious and tender emotions upon this very point: "I *cannot* do it." My soul bleeds for thee, my unhappy! But it must be done, or thou art lost forever. Yet what is the amount of that expression – in the mouth of some a flaunting excuse, and of others, a bitter complaint: "I cannot"? Is the inability to believe in Christ different from an inability to perform any other duty? Is there any harder necessity of calling the God of truth a *liar;* in not believing the record which He hath given of His Son, than of committing any other sin? The inability created, the necessity imposed, by the *enmity* of the carnal mind against God? (Rom. viii. 7) It is the inability of wickedness, and of nothing else. Instead of being an apology, it is itself the essential crime, and can never become its own vindication.

But it is even so. The evil does lie too deep for the reach of human remedies. Yet a remedy there is, and an effectual one. It is here: "I will sprinkle clean water upon you, and ye shall be clean; from all your filthiness and from all your idols will I cleanse you. A new heart also will I give you, and a new spirit will I put within you; and I will take away the stony heart out of your flesh; and I will give you an heart of flesh. And I will put my spirit within you, and cause you to walk in my statutes; and ye shall keep my judgments and do them"(Ezek. xxxvi. 25-27). Try this experiment. Go with thy "filthiness," and thine "idols;" go with thy "stony heart," and thy perverse spirit, which are thy real inability, to God upon the throne of grace; spread out before Him His "exceeding great and precious promises;" importune Him as the hearer of prayer, in the name of Jesus, for the accomplishment of it to thyself. Wait for His mercy, it is worth waiting for, and remember His Word: "Therefore will the Lord wait, that he may be gracious unto you; and therefore will he be exalted, that he may have mercy upon you: for the Lord is a God of judgment; blessed are all they that wait for him.[4]"

5. Finally; from the foregoing principles and considerations, it is evident, that *the great body of Pædobaptist churches have much to reform in regard to their treatment of baptized children, and are bound to address themselves to that reform with all speed and fidelity.* It has been already observed, that one great end for which the Church of God was instituted, was to train up, from age to age, a seed to serve God, and to be faithful witnesses in behalf of the truth and order of His family, in the midst of an unbelieving world. If this be so, then, surely the Church, in her ecclesiastical capacity, is bound carefully to watch over the education, and especially, the religious education of her youthful members; nor is there any risk in asserting, that just in proportion as she has been faithful to this part of her trust, she has flourished in orthodoxy, piety, and peace; and that when she has neglected it, her children have grown up in ignorance, and too often in profligacy, and wandered from her fold into every form of error. If the Church wishes her baptized youth to be a comfort and a strength to their moral mother; if she wishes them to adhere with intelligence, and with dutiful affection to her distinctive testimony; and to be a generation to the praise of Zion's King, when their fathers shall have gone to their final account; then let her, by all means, watch over the training of her young people with peculiar diligence and fidelity; and consider a very large part of her duty, as a church, as consisting in constant and faithful attention to the moral and religious culture of the rising generation.

---

4. The two preceding paragraphs are from the powerful and eloquent pen of the late Rev. J.M. Mason P.P. See *Christian's Magazine,* Vol. II. p. 414-416.

What is the reason that so many of the baptized youth, in almost all our Pædobaptist churches, grow up in ignorance and disregard of the religion of their parents? Why are so many of them, when they come to judge and act for themselves, found embracing systems of gross error, if not total infidelity, and wandering, in too many instances, into the paths of degrading profligacy? It is not enough to say, that our children are by nature depraved, and prone to the ways of error and folly. This is, doubtless, true; but it is not the whole truth. It cannot be questioned, that much of the reason lies at the door of the Church herself, as well as of the parents of such youth. The Church has too often forgotten that baptism is as really a seal to the Church, as it is to the parents and the children who receive it. And, therefore, while in many instances, a superstitious regard has been paid to the mere rite of baptism, a most deplorable neglect of the duties arising from it has been indulged, even by some of our most evangelical churches. Parents, while most vigilantly attentive to the literary, scientific, and ornamental education of their children, have slighted, to a most humiliating degree, their moral and religious training. They have sent them to schools conducted by immoral, heretical, or infidel teachers, who, of course, paid no regard to that part of their education which is unspeakably the most important of all; or who rather might be expected to exert in this respect, a most pestiferous influence. And, after this *cruel treatment of their offspring,* have appeared to be utterly surprised when they turned out profligates! What other result could have been expected?

While it is granted that the primary movements in the great work of Christian education, are to be expected from the parents; – indeed, if the work be not begun on the mother's lap, a most important period has been suffered to pass unimproved; – yet the church has a duty to perform in this matter which is seldom realized. It is hers, by her pastor and eldership, to stimulate and guide parents in this arduous and momentous labour; to see that proper schools for her baptized youth are formed or selected; to put the Bible, and suitable catechisms, and other compends of religious truth into their hands; to convene them at stated intervals for instruction, exhortation, and prayer; to remind them from time to time, with parental tenderness, of their duty to confess Christ, and recognize their relation to His Church by their own personal act; and, if they fall into gross error, or open immorality, or continue to neglect religion, to exercise toward them, with parental affection, and yet with firmness, that discipline which Christ has appointed expressly for the benefit of all the members, and especially of the youthful members of His covenanted family. If this plan were faithfully pursued with our baptized youth, I am constrained to concur with the pious Mr. Baxter in believing, that in nineteen cases out of twenty, our children, consecrated to God in their infancy, would grow up dutiful, sober, orderly, and serious, and before they reached mature age, recognize their membership by a personal act, with sincerity and to edification. Happy era! When shall the Church of God be blessed with such fidelity, and with such results?

CHAPTER THREE

The Mode of Administering Baptism

"Can any man forbid water, that these should not be baptized?" (Acts x. 47).

Having endeavoured, in the preceding discourses, to show that the baptism of infants is a scriptural and reasonable service, I now proceed to inquire into the *mode* in which this ordinance ought to be administered.

And here, it is well known, that there is a very serious diversity of opinion. On the one hand, our Baptist brethren believe that there is no true baptism unless the whole body be plunged under water. While on the other hand, we, and a very great majority of the Christian world, maintain that the mode of baptism by sprinkling or affusion is a method just as valid and lawful as any other. It will be my object, in the present discourse, to support the latter opinion – or rather to maintain, from Scripture, and from the best usage of the Christian Church – that baptism by sprinkling or affusion not only rests on as good authority as immersion, but that it is a method decisively more scriptural, suitable, and edifying.

From the very nature of this subject it will require some little extent of discussion to place it in a proper light, and some closeness of attention to apprehend and follow the arguments which may be employed. Let me then request from you a candid and patient hearing. If I know my own heart, it is my purpose to exhibit the subject in the light of truth; and to advance nothing but that which appears to rest on the authority of Him who instituted the ordinance under consideration, and who is alone competent to declare His will concerning it. And,

1. Let us attend to *the real meaning of the original word which is employed in the New Testament to express this sacramental rite.*

The Greek word βαπιζω which we translate *baptize,* from the circumstance of its having been so constantly and so long the subject of earnest discussion; and from its near resemblance to the English word which we employ to render it (or, we might rather say, its identity with that word), has become so familiar with the public mind, that it may almost be regarded as a naturalized term of our language.

Now, we contend, that this word does not necessarily, nor even commonly, signify to immerse; but also implies to wash, to sprinkle, to pour on water, and to tinge or dye with any liquid; and, therefore, accords very well with the mode of baptism by sprinkling or affusion.

I am aware, indeed, that our Baptist brethren, as before intimated, believe, and confidently assert, that the only legitimate and authorized meaning of this word, is to immerse; and that it is *never* employed, in a single case, in any part of the Bible, to express the application of water in any other manner. I can venture, my friends, to assure you, with the utmost confidence, that this representation is wholly incorrect. I can assure you, that the word which we render *baptize*, does legitimately signify the application of water in any way, as well as by immersion. Nay, I can assure you, if the most mature and competent Greek scholars that ever lived may be allowed to decide in this case, that many examples of the use of this word occur in Scripture, in which it not only *may,* but manifestly *must* signify sprinkling, perfusion, or washing in any way. Without entering into the minute details of Greek criticism in reference to this term, which would be neither suitable to our purpose, nor consistent with our limits; it will suffice to refer to a few of those passages of Scripture which will at once illustrate and confirm the position which I have laid down.

Thus, when the Evangelists tell us that the Scribes and Pharisees invariably "washed (in the original, *baptized*) their hands before dinner;" when we are told that, when they come in from the market, "except they wash, (in the original, 'except they baptize') they eat not;" when we read of the Pharisees being so scrupulous about the "washing (in the original, the *baptizing*) of cups, and pots, and brazen vessels, and tables;" when our Saviour speaks of His disciples being "baptized with the Holy Ghost," in manifest allusion to the pouring out of the Holy Spirit on the day of Pentecost; when John the Baptist predicted, that they should be "baptized with the Holy Ghost, and with fire," in reference to the Holy Ghost sitting upon each of them as with "cloven tongues of fire" on the same day; when we find the apostle representing the children of Israel as all baptized by a cloud passing over without touching them; and also as baptized in the Red Sea, when we know that none of them were immersed in passing through, or, at most, only sprinkled by the spray of the watery walls on each side; for we are expressly told that they went through *"dry shod;"* when Judas, in celebrating the Paschal supper with his Master, in dipping a morsel of bread on a bunch of herbs in the "sop" in the dish, is said, by Christ Himself, to baptize his hand in the dish" (as it is in the original, Matt. xxvi. 23), which no one can imagine implies the immersion of His whole hand in the gravy of which they were all partaking; I say, when the word "baptize" is used in these and similar senses, it surely cannot mean in any of these cases to immerse or plunge. If a man is said by the inspired Evangelist to be baptized, when his hands only are washed; and if "tables" (or couches, on which they reclined at meals, as appears from the original) are spoken of as "baptized," when the cleansing of water was applied to them in any manner, and when the complete immersion of them in water is out of the question; surely nothing can be plainer than that the Holy Spirit who endited the Scriptures, does not restrict the meaning of this word to the idea of plunging, or total immersion.

Again; the New Testament meaning of this term appears

from the manner in which it is applied to the ablutions of the cere-monial economy. The apostle, in writing to the Hebrews, and speaking of the Jewish ritual, says, "It stood only in meats and drinks and divers washings" (in the original, "divers baptisms"). Now we know that by far the greater part of these "divers washings" were accomplished by sprinkling and allusion, and not by immersion. The blood of the Paschal Lamb was directed to be "sprinkled" on the door-posts of the Israelites, as a token of Jeho-vah's favour, and of protection from death. When they entered into covenant with God at Sinai, their solemn vows were directed to be scaled by a similar sign. After Moses had spoken every precept to all the people according to the law, and they had given their consent, and promised to obey, he took the blood of the sacrifice, and water, and "sprinkled" both the book and the peo-ple (Heb. ix. 19). On the great day of atonement, when the High Priest went into the most Holy Place, he "sprinkled" the blood of the sacrifice on the Mercy Seat, as a token of propitiation and cleansing. When any individual was to be cleansed, and delivered from legal guilt, the blood of the sacrifice was to be "sprinkled" upon him seven times. In like manner at other times, the conse-crated oil was to be sprinkled upon him who applied for deliver-ance from pollution.

Thus the people were to be ceremonially delivered from their uncleanness.[1] When Aaron and his sons were set apart to their office, they were sprinkled with blood, as a sign of purifica-tion. When tents or dwelling houses were to be cleansed from pollution, it was done, among other things, by sprinkling them with water. When the vessels, used in domestic economy, were to be ceremonially cleansed, the object was effected in the same manner, by sprinkling them with water.[2] In a few cases, and but a few, the mode of cleansing by plunging into water is prescribed.

---

1. See Exodus, xxix. 40; Leviticus, i. 3, 4, 5, 8, 9. 14 and 15 chapters; Numbers, 19th chapter, and Deuteronomy, 12th and 15th chapters.

2. See Numbers, xix. 17-22.

Now, these are the "divers baptisms" of which the apostle speaks. It is worthy of notice that they are *divers* (διαφοροις). If they had been of one kind – immersion only – this term could not with propriety have been used. But they were of different kinds – some sprinkling, others pouring, some scouring and rinsing, (see Leviticus vi. 28.) and some plunging; but all pronounced by the inspired apostle to be baptism.

But, happily, the inspired apostle does not leave us in doubt what those "divers baptisms" were, of which he speaks. He singles out and presents sprinkling as his chosen and only specimen. "For (says he, in the 13th 19th and 21st verses of the same chapter, explaining what he means by 'divers baptisms'), if the blood of bulls, and of goats, and the ashes of an heifer, *sprinkling* the unclean, sanctifieth to the purifying of the flesh; how much more shall the blood of Christ, &c. For when Moses had spoken every precept to all the people, according to the law, he took the blood of calves and of goats, with water, and scarlet wool, and hyssop, and *sprinkled* both the book and all the people. Moreover, he *sprinkled* likewise with blood both the tabernacle, and all the vessels of the ministry." If the apostle understood his own meaning, then, it is manifest that in speaking of "divers baptisms," he had a principal reference to the application of blood and of water by *sprinkling*.

In short, it is perfectly manifest, to every one competent to judge in the case, that the Greek words which we translate *baptize* and *baptism*, do undoubtedly signify, in a number of cases, in both the Old and New Testaments, the washing with water, or the application of water in any way. To immerse, is, undoubtedly, one of the senses which may be applied to the words. But it is so far from being the universal, the necessary meaning, as our Baptist brethren assert, that it is not even the common meaning. And I am well persuaded that the venerable Dr. Owen, certainly one of the greatest and best men of the day in which he lived, is borne out by truth when he pronounces, "That no one instance can be given in Scripture, in which the word which we render baptize, does necessarily signify either to dip or plunge." In every case the word admits of a different sense; and it is really imposing on public credulity to insist that it always does, and necessarily must signify immersion.[3]

In like manner, if we examine the senses manifestly attached to βαπτω and βαπτιζω, by the best Greek classical writers, as shown by the ablest lexicographers and critics, the same result will be established; in other words, it will appear that these words are used, and often used, to express the ideas of cleansing, pouring, washing, wetting, and tinging, or dyeing, as well as immersion: and, of course, that no certain evidence in favour of the doctrine of our Baptist brethren, can be derived from this source. Indeed, a late eminent Antipædobaptist writer, while he strenuously maintains that βαπτιζω always signifies to immerse, acknowledges that he has "all the lexicographers and commentators against him in that opinion."[4] How far the confidence which, in the face of this acknowledgment, he expresses, that they are *all wrong,* and that his interpretation alone is right, is either modest or well-founded, must be left to the impartial reader.

It is evident, then, that our Baptist brethren can gain nothing by an appeal to the original word employed in the New Testament to express this ordinance. It decides nothing. All impartial judges – by which I mean all the most profound and mature Greek scholars, who are neither theologians nor sectarians – agree in pronouncing, that the term in question imports the application of water by sprinkling, pouring, tinging, wetting, or in any other way, as well as by plunging the whole body under it.

2. There is *nothing in the thing signified by baptism which renders immersion more necessary or proper than any other mode of applying water in this ordinance.*

Our Baptist brethren suppose and insist that there is some-

3. See this point set in a clear and strong light by the Rev. Dr. Woods, in his *Lectures on Infant Baptism*; by the Rev. Professor Stuart, in the *Biblical Repository*, No, 10; by the Rev. Professor Pond, of Maine, in his *Treatise on Christian Baptism*; in the *Biblical Repertory*, Vol. III, p. 475, &c. &c.

4. Carson, *Baptism in Its Mode and Subjects*, p. 79.

thing in the emblematical meaning of baptism, which renders dipping or plunging the only proper mode of administering the ordinance. And hence nothing is more common, among the brethren of that denomination, than to pour ridicule on all other modes of baptizing, as entirely deficient in meaning and expressiveness. I am persuaded, my friends, that the slightest examination of the subject will convince every impartial inquirer that there is no solid ground for this representation.

It is granted, on all hands, that the thing principally signified by baptism, is the renovation and sanctification of the heart, by the cleansing influences of the Holy Spirit. This was, undoubtedly, the blessing of which circumcision was an emblem. It signified, as the inspired apostle tells us, "the putting off the body of the sins of the flesh."[5] "He is not a Jew," says the same apostle, "who is one outwardly; neither is that circumcision which is outward in the flesh; but he is a Jew which is one inwardly; and circumcision is that of the heart, in the Spirit, and not in the letter."[6] In like manner, baptism signifies the renovation of the heart by the special operation of the Spirit of God. It is intended ever to keep us in mind, by a very significant and striking emblem, that we are all by nature polluted and guilty, and that we stand in need of the pardoning and purifying grace of God by a crucified Redeemer.

Now, when the inspired writers speak of imparting the influences of the Holy Spirit to the children of men, by what kind of figure is that blessing commonly expressed? I answer – as every one who is familiar with the Bible will concur in answering – much more frequently by sprinkling and pouring out, than by any other form of expression. Thus the prophet Isaiah speaks again and again of the Spirit being poured out upon the people from on high.[7] Take a single specimen – I will pour water upon

---

5. Colossians, ii. 11.

6. Romans, ii. 28, 29.

7. Isaiah, xxxii. 15; xliv. 3.

him that is thirsty, and floods upon the dry ground I will pour my spirit upon thy seed, and my blessing upon thine offspring." The prophets, Ezekiel, Joel, and Zechariah, repeatedly employ the same language;[8] and this form of expression is also found more than once in the New Testament.[9] Indeed it seems to be the favourite language of the Spirit of God when speaking on this subject. In other places the term sprinkling is employed to express the same idea. Accordingly, Jehovah says, by the prophet Ezekiel, "I will sprinkle clean water upon you, and ye shall be clean from all your filthiness, and from all your idols will I cleanse you. A new heart also will I give you, and a new spirit will I put within you; and I will take away the stony heart out of your flesh, and I will give you an heart of flesh."[10] And, in like manner, the prophet Isaiah, when speaking of the coming of the Messiah, and the benefits accruing to the Church in New Testament times, foretells – "So shall he sprinkle many nations."[11] Again, this divine sanctifying influence in its application to men, is represented by the Psalmist, and by the prophet Hosea, under the similitude of rain, which we know descends in drops, sprinkling the earth, and its verdant furniture.[12] "He shall come down like rain upon the mown grass; as showers that water the earth."

But to come still nearer to the point in hand. We have not only seen that whenever the inspired writers wish to express the idea of the Holy Spirit being imparted to men, either to sanctify their hearts, or to furnish them with miraculous powers, the figure of "pouring out" is, in almost all cases, adopted, and that of immersion *never;* but, further, when they use the specific term which expresses the ordinance before us; when they speak of the "baptism of the Spirit," how do they explain it? Hear the explana-

---

8. Ezekiel, xxxix. 29. Joel, ii. 28, 29. Zechariah, xii. 10.

9. Acts, ii. 17, 18; x. 45.

10. Ezekiel, xxxvi. 25, 26.

11. Ezek. lii. 15.

12. Psalm, lxxii. 6. Hosea, vi. 3.

tion by the Master Himself. The Saviour, after His resurrection, told His disciples, that "John truly baptized with water, but they should be baptized with the Holy Ghost" not many days from that time (Acts i. 4, 5), and directing them to remain in Jerusalem until this promise should be fulfilled on the day of Pentecost. And how did the Holy Spirit baptize the people then? By immersion? Not at all; but by being "poured out." Accordingly, the apostle Peter, in giving an account to his brethren of what occurred in the house of Cornelius, declares: "And as I began to speak, the Holy Ghost fell on them, *as on us at the beginning,* (that is at the beginning of the New Testament economy, on the day of Pentecost.) Then remembered I the words of the Lord, how he said, John, indeed baptized with water; but ye shall be baptized with the Holy Ghost" (Acts xi. 15, 16). The *baptism of the Holy Ghost,* then, consisted in the *pouring out,* or *effusion* of the Holy Ghost. This was the baptism predicted by the prophets. This was the baptism which our Lord himself promised. And this was the baptism realized on the day of Pentecost. I ask, again, was this immersion? Yet it was baptism. And here, we may add, is an indubitable example of the word *baptism* being used in a sense which cannot possibly imply immersion.

Surely it is not without design or meaning, that we find language of this kind so generally, I might almost say, so uniformly used. Can a single instance be produced from the Word of God in which the cleansing influences of the Holy Spirit are symbolized by dipping or plunging into, water, or into oil or blood? Or can a single example be found in which believers are represented as being dipped or plunged into the Holy Ghost! No such example is recollected. Whenever the inspired writers speak of the Holy Spirit being imparted to the children of men, either in His sanctifying power, or His miraculous gifts, they never represent the benefit under the figure of immersion; but always, unless my memory deceives me, by the figures of "sprinkling," "pouring out," "falling," or "resting upon" from on high. Now, if baptism, so far as it has a symbolical meaning, is intended to represent the cleansing of the Holy Spirit, as all agree, it is evident that no mode of applying the baptismal water can be more strikingly adapted to convey its symbolical meaning, or more strongly expressive of the great benefit which the ordinance is intended to hold forth and seal, than sprinkling or pouring. Nay, is it not manifest that this mode of administering the ordinance, is *far more* in accordance with Bible language, and Bible allusion, than any other? Surely, then, baptism by sprinkling or affusion, would have been treated with less scorn by our Baptist brethren, if they had recollected that these are, invariably, the favourite figures of the inspired writers when they speak of the richest covenant blessings which the Spirit of God imparts to His beloved people. Surely all attempts to turn this mode of applying the sacramental water in baptism into ridicule, is really nothing less than shameless ridicule of the statements and the language of God's own Word!

3. The *circumstances attending the several cases of baptism recorded in the New Testament, render it highly probable, not to say morally certain, that the immersion of the whole body could not have been the mode of baptism then commonly adopted.*

The baptism of the three thousand converts made by the instrumentality of Peter's preaching, on the day of Pentecost, is the first remarkable instance of Christian baptism which occurs in the New Testament history. Christ had promised, before He left His disciples, that He would send to them His Holy Spirit, and the favourite expression by which He was accustomed to designate this gift, was that He would *pour out* the Holy Spirit upon them. Accordingly, in ten days after His ascension to heaven, He was pleased, in a most extraordinary manner, to fulfill His promise. The Spirit was poured out with a power unknown before. And, what is remarkable, the apostle Peter assures the assembled multitude, that what they then witnessed was a fulfillment of the prediction by the prophet Joel, that the Holy Spirit should be imparted in a manner prefigured by the term *pouring out,* or affusion. Three thousand were converted under the overwhelming impression of divine truth, dispensed in a single sermon; and were all baptized, and "added to the church" in a single day. From the short account given of this wonderful transaction, we gather, that the multitude on whom this impression was made, was convened in some part of the temple. They seem to have come together about the third hour of the day, that is, nine o'clock in the morning, according to the Jewish mode of computing time. At least, when Peter rose to commence his sermon,, that was the hour. Besides the discourse of which we have a sketch in the chapter containing the account, we are told he exhorted and testified with many other words. All these services, together with receiving the confession of three thousand converts, must unavoidably have consumed several hours; leaving only four or five hours, at the utmost, for baptizing the whole number. But they were all baptized that same day. We read nothing, however, of the apostles taking the converts away from "Solomon's Porch," or wherever else they were assembled, to any river or stream for the sake of baptizing them. Indeed, at that season of the year, there was no river or brook in the immediate neighbourhood of Jerusalem, which would admit of immersing a human being. Besides, is it likely that this great multitude, most of whom were probably strangers in Jerusalem, could have been furnished with such a change of raiment as health and decorum required; or that they could have been baptized without clothing altogether; or remained on the ground, through the public exercises, in their wet clothes? Surely all these suppositions are so utterly improbable that they may be confidently rejected. But, above all, was it physically possible supposing all the apostles to have officiated in the administration of this ordinance, for twelve men to have immersed three thousand persons in four or five hours; which we have seen must have been the case, if, as is evident, the preaching, the examination of candidates, and the baptizing of the whole number took place after nine o'clock in the forenoon? Those who have witnessed a series of baptisms by immersion know how arduous and exhausting is the bodily effort which it requires. To immerse a single person, with due decorum and solemnity, will undoubtedly require from five to six minutes. Of course, to immerse one hundred, would consume, at this rate, between nine and ten hours. Now, even if so much time could possibly be assigned to this part of the work, on the same day, which is plainly inadmissible, can we suppose that the twelve apostles stood, for nine or ten hours, themselves, in the water, constantly engaged in a series of efforts among the most severe and exhausting to human strength that can well be undertaken?[13] To imagine this, would be among the most improbable, not to say extravagant imaginations that could be formed on such a subject. Yet even this supposition, unreasonable as it is, falls far short of providing for even one half of the requisite number. The man, therefore, who can believe that the three thousand on the day of Pentecost were baptized by immersion, must have great faith, and a wonderful facility in accommodating his belief to his wishes.

With regard to the baptism of John, many of the same remarks are entirely applicable. Our Baptist brethren universally take for granted that John's baptism was performed by immersion; and on the ground of that assumption, they speak with great confidence of their mode of baptism as the only lawful mode. Now, even if it were certain that the forerunner of Christ had always baptized by immersion, still it would be little to the purpose, since it is plain that John's baptism was not Christian baptism. Had this been the case, then, it is evident, that a large part of the population of "Jerusalem and Judea, and of the region round about Jordan," would have been professing Christians. But was it so? Every reader of the New Testament history knows it was not; that, on the contrary, it is apparent from the whole narrative, that a great majority of those whom John baptized, contin-

---

13. "A gentleman of veracity told the writer, that he was once present when *forty-seven* were dipped in one day, in the usual way. The first operator began, and went through the ceremony, until be had dipped *twenty-five* persons; when he was so fatigued, that he was compelled to give it up to the other, who with great apparent difficulty dipped the other *twenty-two*. Both appeared completely exhausted, and went off the ground into a house hard by, to change their clothes and refresh themselves." *Scripture Directory for Baptism by a Layman,* 14.

ued to stand aloof from the Saviour. But what decides this point, beyond the possibility of appeal or cavil, is the statement in the nineteenth chapter of the Acts of the Apostles, where we are told that some who had received John's baptism, were afterwards baptized in the name of the Lord Jesus. Some opponents of this conclusion have suggested that in the narrative given of this transaction (Acts xix. 1-6), we are to consider the 5th verse, not as the language of the inspired historian, but as a continuation of Paul's discourse, as recorded in the 4th verse. Professor Stuart, in his remarks on the "Mode of Baptism," in the *Biblical Repository* (No. X. 386), has shown conclusively that this gloss is wholly inadmissible; and even leads to the most evident absurdity. But there is no evidence, and I will venture to say, no probability, that John ever baptized by immersion. The evangelists informs us that he baptized *great multitudes.* It appears, as before suggested, that "all Jerusalem, and all Judea, and the region round about Jordan," flocked to his ministry, and "were baptized of him in Jordan, confessing their sins." Some have supposed that he baptized *two* millions of people. But suppose the number to be one-twentieth part of this computation. The smallest estimate that we can consider as answering the description of the inspired historians is that he baptized one hundred thousand individuals. And this, in about one year and a half. That is, he must have immersed nearly two hundred, upon an average, every day, during the whole of the period in question. Now, I ask, is it possible for human strength, day after day, for more than five hundred days together, to undergo such labour? It cannot be imagined. The thing is not merely improbable; it is impossible. To accomplish so much, it would have been necessary that the zealous Baptist should spend the whole of every day standing in the water, for a year and a half, and even this would have failed altogether of being sufficient. I say again, with confidence, it is impossible.

But that John baptized by immersion is utterly incredible on another account. Can we imagine that so great a multitude could have been provided on the spot with convenient changes of raiment to admit of their being plunged consistently with their health? Or can we suppose that the greater part of their number, would remain for hours on the ground in their wet clothes? And if not, would decency have permitted multitudes of both sexes to appear, and to undergo the administration of the ordinance in that mode, in a state of entire nakedness? Surely we need not wait for an answer. Neither supposition is admissible.

Nor is this reasoning at all invalidated by the statement of one of the evangelists, that John "baptized at Enon, near Salem, because there was much water there;" or, as it is in the original, "because there were *many waters* there. For, independently of immersion altogether, plentiful streams of water were absolutely necessary for the constant refreshment and sustenance of the many thousands who were encamped from day to day, to witness the preaching and the baptism of this extraordinary man; together with the beasts employed for their transportation. Only figure to yourselves a large encampment of men, women, and children, consisting almost continually of many thousand souls, continuing together for a number of days in succession; constantly coming and going; and all this in a warm climate, where springs and wells of water were comparatively rare and precious; only figure to yourselves such an assemblage, and such a scene, and you will be at no loss to perceive why it was judged important to convene them near the banks of abundant streams of water. Had not this been done, they must, in a few hours, have either quitted the ground, or suffered real distress.

It is evident, then, that often and confidently as the baptism of John has been cited as conclusive, in favour of immersion, it cannot be considered as affording the least solid ground for such a conclusion. There is not the smallest probability that he ever baptized an individual in this manner. As a poor man, who lived in the wilderness; whose raiment was of the meanest kind; and whose food was such alone as the desert afforded; it is not to be supposed that he possessed appropriate vessels, for administering baptism to multitudes by pouring or sprinkling. He, therefore, seems to have made use of the neighbouring stream of water for this purpose, descending its banks, and setting his feet on its margin, so as to admit of his using a handful, to answer the symbolical purpose intended by the application of water in baptism.

The circumstances attending the baptism of our blessed Saviour by John, have been often adduced by our Baptist brethren as strongly favouring the practice of immersion; but when they are examined, they will be found to afford no real aid to that cause. In our common translation, indeed, the Evangelist Matthew tells us (ch. iii. 16), that Jesus, when He was baptized, went up straightway out of the water, &c.; and the Evangelist Mark tells us (ch. i. 9, 10), that Jesus was baptized of John in Jordan; "and straightway, coming up out of the water, he saw the heavens opened," &c. This is considered by many superficial readers as decisive in establishing the fact that immersion must have been used on that occasion; but the moment we look into the original, it becomes evident that the language of both the Evangelists imports only that Jesus, after He was baptized, went up from the water, that is, ascended the banks from the river. Nothing more is, unquestionably, imported by the terms used; and this leaves the mode of administering the ordinance altogether undecided. Laying aside His sandals, He might only have stepped a few inches into the river, or He might have gone merely to the water's edge, without stepping into it at all.[14]

The baptism of Paul, by Ananias, is another of the scriptural examples of the administration of the ordinance in question, which yet affords not the smallest hint or presumption in favour of immersion; but rather the contrary.

We are told that Paul, the infuriated persecutor, while "breathing out threatenings and slaughter against the disciples of the Lord," was met on His way to Damascus, and by the mighty power of the Saviour whom he persecuted, was stricken down, and fell prostrate and blind to the ground. In this feeble state he was lifted up, and "led by the hand, and carried into Damascus;

---

14. See a very luminous and satisfactory view of the record of this baptism, by Professor Stuart, of Andover, in the *Biblical Repository*, No. X, p. 319, 320.

and he was there three days without sight, and did neither eat nor drink." In these circumstances, Ananias, a servant of God, is directed to go to him, and teach him what to do. "And Ananias," we are told, "went his way, and entered into the house; and putting his hands on him, said, Brother Saul, the Lord, even Jesus, that appeared unto thee in the way, as thou camest, hath sent me, that thou mightest receive thy sight, and be filled with the Holy Ghost. And now, why tarriest thou? Arise, and be baptized, and wash away thy sins, calling on the name of the Lord. And immediately there fell from his eyes as it had been scales; and he received sight forthwith, and arose, and was baptized. And when he had received meat he was strengthened."[15]

The attentive reader will, no doubt, take notice that in this narrative there is not a single turn of expression which looks like baptizing by immersion. There is no hint that Paul changed his raiment; or that he and Ananias went out of the house to a neighbouring pond or stream. On the contrary, every part of the statement wears a different aspect. Paul, when Ananias went to him, was evidently extremely feeble. He was sitting or lying in the house, perfectly blind, and having taken no sustenance for three days. Can it be imagined that a wise and humane man, in these circumstances, would have had him carried forth, and plunged into cold water, which, in his exhausted state, would have been equally distressing and dangerous? It cannot be for a moment supposed. Nothing like it is hinted. Ananias simply directs him to "stand up and be baptized." "And immediately there fell from his eyes as it had been scales; and he received sight forthwith, and arose, and was baptized." It was after the baptism, as we learn, that he received sustenance and was "strengthened." It would really seem as if no impartial reader could receive any other impression from this account, than that Paul *stood up*, in the apartment, in which Ananias found him, and there received baptism by pouring or sprinkling on him a small quantity of that water which

---

15. Acts, ix. and xxii. compared.

is applied in this ordinance as a symbol of spiritual cleansing.

Again, the baptism of the Ethiopian eunuch, when duly considered, will be found equally remote from affording the smallest countenance to that conclusion in favour of immersion, which has been so often and so confidently drawn from it.

The eunuch was travelling on the public highway, when Philip met him. They had been reading and commenting on a prophecy of the Messiah, in which mention is made of His *sprinkling many nations.* When they came to a rivulet of water, the eunuch said, "See, here is water, what doth hinder me to be baptized?" Philip had, no doubt, been explaining to him the nature, design, and obligation of this ordinance, or he would not have been likely to ask such a question. The servant of God consented to baptize him; and, as they were travelling, and probably destitute of any convenient vessel for dipping up a portion of water from the stream, they both went down to the water, probably no further than to its margin; far enough to take up a small portion of it to sprinkle or pour on the eunuch. The narrative, in the original, ascertains nothing more than that they both went to and from the water. In our translation, indeed, it is said, they both went down into the water, and came up out of the water. But, when we look into the original text, we find the strict meaning of the terms employed to be, that Philip and the eunuch went down the banks to the water, and coming from the water, reascended the banks again, to the place where the chariot in which they rode had been left. The same form of expression is used as in the case of Peter and the tribute money, "Go thou to the sea, and cast an hook," &c. (Matt. xvii. 27). Here we cannot suppose that our Lord meant to command Peter to plunge into the sea, but only to go to the water's edge, and cast in a hook. The same form of expression is also employed in many other passages of the New Testament, where immersion is wholly out of the question: As in John. ii. 12, where it is said, Jesus "went down to Capernaum;" Acts vii. 15, Jacob "went down into Egypt;" Acts xviii. 22, He "went down to Antioch," &c. Surely, no one will dream of immersion in any of these cases. There is nothing, then, in any of the language here used, which necessarily, or even probably, implies immersion. At any rate, the terms employed apply equally to both. There is the same evidence that Philip was plunged, as that the eunuch was. It is said they both went to the water. Nor can we consider it as at all likely that, in the circumstances in which they were placed as travellers, they were either of them immersed. It is plain, therefore, that all the confidence which our Baptist brethren have so often expressed, that the case of the Ethiopian eunuch is a certain example of immersion, must be regarded as presenting no solid evidence in their favour, and as really amounting to a gross imposition on popular credulity.

The next remarkable instance of baptism recorded in the New Testament, is that of Cornelius and his household. Cornelius, a "devout man, who feared God," was directed, in a vision, to send for Peter, the apostle, who should impart to him the knowledge of the Gospel of Christ. Peter, on his arrival, having ascertained wherefore Cornelius had sent for him, unfolded to him, and to all who were convened in his house, the way of salvation. "While he was yet speaking, the Holy Ghost fell upon all of them which heard the word. Then answered Peter, Can any man forbid water, that these should not be baptized, who have received the Holy Ghost as well as we? And he commanded them to be baptized in the name of the Lord."

In this passage, there is nothing that has the remotest appearance of immersion. No hint is given of the candidates for baptism being led out of the house to a river or pool for the purpose of being dipped. The language of Peter has an entirely different aspect: *"Can any man forbid water,* that these should not be baptized?" That is, "Can any man forbid water being brought in a convenient vessel, to be applied by pouring or sprinkling?" He had just spoken of the Holy Ghost being poured out upon them; and what could be more natural than that he should apply water, the emblem of spiritual cleansing, in conformity with the same striking figure? They were not dipped into the Holy Ghost; but the Holy Ghost was poured upon them. They were not applied to the Holy Ghost; but the Holy Ghost was applied to them.

He "fell upon them;" and the introduction of water, to be applied in a corresponding manner, was immediately authorized.

The baptism of the jailer and his household, at Philippi, still more decisively leads to the same conclusion. If we examine the circumstances which attended this baptism, they will be found to preclude, not merely the probability, but I may say with confidence, the possibility of its having been performed by immersion. Paul and Silas were closely confined in prison when this solemn service was performed. While they were engaged in "praying and singing praises to God," a great earthquake shook the prison to its foundation, and the bonds of the prisoners were immediately unloosed. The jailer, awaking from his sleep, called for a light, and sprang in, and came trembling, and fell down before Paul and Silas, and said, "Sirs, what must I do to be saved?" And they said, "Believe on the Lord Jesus Christ, and thou shalt be saved, and thy house. And they spake unto him the word, and to all that were in his house. And he took them the same hour of the night, and washed their stripes, and was baptized, he and all his, straightway." This whole transaction, you will observe, occurred a little after midnight, and in a prison – that is, in the outer prison; for the jailer seems to have brought them out of the dungeon, or "inner prison," into some other apartment of the edifice. For it was not until next morning, some hours after the baptism, that the magistrates gave the keeper permission to let them out of the prison. He and his family were evidently baptized "the same hour of the night," that is, between midnight, when we are expressly told the earthquake occurred, and day; and while yet in the place of confinement. Now, I ask, how can we imagine it possible that the jailer and his family should be baptized by immersion, in the circumstances in which they were placed? We cannot suppose that there was a river, or a pool of water, or a baptistery within the walls of the prison, adapted to meet an occasion as unexpected as any thing could be, which had never occurred there before, and was never likely to occur in like circumstances again. He who can believe this, must be ready to adopt any supposition, however extravagant, for the sake of an hypothesis. As little can we imagine that Paul and Silas would be dishonest enough to steal out of the prison by night, and accompany the jailer and his family to the river which runs near the city of Philippi, for the purpose of plunging them; especially as we know, on the one hand, how backward they were, the next morning, to quit the prison, unless brought out by the magistrates who had illegally imprisoned them; and, on the other hand, how much terrified the jailer was at the thought of the prisoners escaping from confinement, and of his being responsible, even with his own life, for their safe keeping.

In like manner, we might go over all the other cases of baptism recorded in the New Testament, and show that, in no one case, have we any evidence that the ordinance was administered by immersion. Now, as the disciples of Christ baptized such great multitudes – even more, at one period than John; can we imagine, if the constant, or even the common mode of baptizing had been by plunging the whole body under water, and especially, if they had laid great stress on adherence to this mode; can we imagine, I say, that amidst so many cases of baptism, some term of expression, some incidental circumstance would not have occurred, from which the fact of immersion might have been clearly manifested, or irresistibly inferred? One thing is certain. The inspired writers of the New Testament could not possibly have regarded immersion in baptism in the same light in which it is regarded by our Baptist brethren. The latter, consider their mode of applying water, as essential to the ordinance. They dwell upon it with unceasing fondness; introduce it into every discussion; and lose no opportunity of recommending and urging it as that, without which an alleged baptism is a nullity; nay, an offence to the Head of the Church. While the former, though speaking, directly or indirectly on the subject, in almost every page of the New Testament, and under a great variety of aspects, have not stated a single fact, or employed a single term, which evinces that they either preferred or practised immersion in any case. They have stated, indeed, some facts which can scarcely, by possibility, be reconciled with immersion; but in no instance, have they made a representation which is not entirely reconcilable with the practice of perfusion or sprinkling. On the supposition that the doctrine of our Baptist brethren is true, this is a most unaccountable fact! What! not one evangelist or apostle – though taught by the Spirit of God what to say – kind enough, or wise enough, to put this matter beyond a doubt! The unavoidable inference is, that the inspired writers did not deem the mode of applying water in baptism an essential matter; and did not think it necessary to state it precisely; and, of course, that they differed entirely from our Baptist brethren.

4. Even if it could be proved (which we know it cannot be,) that the mode of baptism adopted in the time of Christ and His apostles, was that of immersion; yet if that method of administering the ordinance were not significant of some truth, which the other modes cannot represent, we are plainly at liberty to regard it as a non-essential circumstance, from which we may depart when expediency requires it, as we are all wont to do in other cases, even with respect to positive institutions. For example, the Lord's Supper was, no doubt, originally instituted with unleavened bread; and this was, probably, at first, the common custom. But as being leavened or unleavened had nothing to do with the design and scope of the ordinance; as bread of either kind is equally emblematical of that spiritual nourishment which it is intended to represent; most professing Christians, and our Baptist brethren among the rest, feel authorized to celebrate the Lord's Supper with leavened bread without the smallest scruple.

Again: the manner of sitting at the Lord's Supper, was, in conformity with the then prevailing posture at feasts, to recline on the elbow on a couch. There can be no doubt that this was the uniform posture at the convivial table at that time; and in the narratives of the evangelists, we have abundant evidence that the same posture was adopted by our blessed Lord in the institution of the sacramental Supper. But as it was only a circumstance connected with the habits of those days, we do not feel bound; and our Baptist brethren among others, do not feel bound, in administering this ordinance, to conform to the original mode. We consider the sacrament as completely and validly dispensed, if bread and wine be reverently received, in commemoration of the Saviour's death, with any posture of the body. Nay, the example of our Saviour Himself, plainly shows that, under a change of circumstances, non-essential modes, originally used, may be dispensed with. The prescribed ritual of the Passover required that the lamb should be eaten with shoes on the feet, and with staves in the hand; but this custom was not followed by Him or His disciples, and, perhaps, never was observed after the entrance into Canaan. But was the Passover rendered either less perfect, or less useful, for all practical purposes, by this omission? Surely we need not wait for an answer.

Now, unless it can be proved, that plunging the body into water, and lifting it out again, was designed to be emblematical of something which cannot be otherwise expressed, we have full liberty, given us by the example of our Lord Himself, to consider this mode as an unimportant circumstance. If the cleansing element of water be applied, in any reverential mode, to the human body, the whole symbolical expression of the ordinance is attained, provided convenience and decorum be duly consulted. If the cleansing or purifying quality of the element used be the idea intended to be set forth in the emblem; and if the greater part, as we have seen, of the typical purifications prescribed under the ceremonial economy were effected by sprinkling; it is plain that the emblem is complete, however the cleansing element may be applied.

CHAPTER FOUR

The Mode of Administering
Baptism, continued

"Can any man forbid water, that these should not be baptized?" Acts x. 47.

5. The *difficulties attending the administration of baptism by immersion, in many cases,* ought to satisfy us that this mode of administering the ordinance cannot be the *only* valid mode, and is not the most *proper* and *edifying* mode.

It is perfectly evident, to every reflecting mind, that the obstacles which may be conceived, and which very frequently, in fact, occur, to render baptism by immersion difficult, if not impracticable, are very many, and very serious. It will be sufficient to hint at a few of the more familiar and obvious. It is well known that some very large districts of country, in various parts of our globe, are so parched and dry, and streams of water so rare, or rather, in many cases, so unknown, for many miles together, that the means of immersing a human body, in any natural stream or pool of water, cannot possibly be obtained but with great trouble and expense; a trouble and expense impracticable to a large portion of every community inhabiting those countries. There are other parts of our globe, near the polar regions, where, during the major portion of every year, the constant reign of severe frost, seals up every natural stream and fountain, and renders the immersion of a human body not merely difficult, but impracticable, without great labour and cost. Nor is this all; even in the temperate and well watered latitudes, there are seasons of the year, often of four or five month's continuance, when baptism by immersion is generally dangerous, and, in many cases, highly so, to the health, and even the lives of both those who administer, and those who receive the ordinance.[1] And, finally, at all seasons, persons labouring under disease, can never be baptized in this mode, with safety, at all; and, of course, must be deprived entirely of the privilege of receiving this seal of the Christian covenant, so reasonable in itself, and so gratifying to the pious mind. It is also certain, that Baptist ministers who are aged and infirm, can never safely officiate in baptizing in any case; and when they are men remarkably frail and feeble in body, they can never undertake, without manifest danger, to baptize individuals of large stature, or more than common corpulency. To all which may be added,

---

1. The Rev. Dr. Austin, in his answer to Mr. Merrill, speaks thus: "In besieged cities, where there are thousands, and hundreds of thousands of people; in sandy deserts, like those of Africa, Arabia, and Palestine; in the northern regions, where the streams, if there be any, are shut up with impenetrable ice; and in severe and extensive droughts, like that which took place in the time of Ahab; sufficiency of water for animal subsistence is scarcely to be procured. Now, suppose God should, according to His predictions, pour out plentiful effusions of His Spirit, so that all the inhabitants of one of these regions or cities, should be born in a day. Upon the Baptist hypothesis, there is an absolute impossibility that they should be baptized, while there is this scarcity of water; and this may last as long as they live." p. 41. So also, Mr. Walker, in his *Doctrine of Baptisms* (chapter 10), speaks of a Jew, who, while travelling with Christians, in the time of Marcus Aurelius Antoninus, about sixty or seventy years after the apostles, was converted, fell sick, and desired baptism. Not having water, they sprinkled him thrice with sand, in the name of the Father, the Son, and the Holy Ghost. He recovered, and his case was reported to the bishop, (or pastor, there being no prelates then) who decided that *the man was baptized, (si modo aqua denuo perfunderatur)* if he only had water poured on him again." This record shows, not merely that the "difficulties" referred to, are far from being ideal; but also that when the defect of the baptism by sand was attempted to be supplied, it was not by any sort of immersion, but only by the pouring on of water.

that the public baptism of females, with all the delicacy and care which can possibly be employed, is certainly, as thousands attest, a practice little in keeping with those religious feelings and impressions with which it is desirable that every Christian solemnity should be attended.

Now, contrast all these difficulties, which, surely form a mass of no small magnitude, with the entire absence of every difficulty in baptizing by sprinkling or affusion. According to our plan, which, we have no doubt, is by far the most scriptural and edifying, baptism may be performed with equal ease and convenience in all countries; at all seasons of the year; in all situations of health or sickness; with equal safety by all ministers, whether young or old, athletic or feeble; and in all circumstances that can well be conceived. how admirably does this accord with the Gospel economy, which is not intended to be confined to any one people, or to any particular climate; but is equally adapted, in all its principles, and in all its rites to every "kindred, and people, and nation, and tongue"!

Accordingly, it is a notorious fact, that, in consideration of the difficulties which have been mentioned as attending immersion, a large body of Baptists in Holland (I mean the Mennonites), who were once warm and uncompromising contenders for this mode of administering baptism, at length gave it up, and, while they still baptize none but adults, have been, for more than a hundred years, in the practice of pouring water on the head of the candidate, through the hand of the administrator. They found that when candidates for baptism were lying on sick beds; or confined in prison; or in a state of peculiarly delicate health; or in various other unusual situations, which may be easily imagined; there was so much difficulty, not to say, in some cases, a total impossibility in baptizing by plunging; that they deliberately, as a denomination, after the death of their first leader, agreed to lay aside, as I said, the practice of immersion, and substituted the plan of affusion.

There is one difficulty more, in reference to the mode of baptism by immersion, of which it is not easy to speak, on an occasion like the present, without appearing to intend ridicule of an ordinance so solemn and important. Fidelity to the subject, however, demands that I speak of it; and I trust no one will suspect me of a design to make any other than a perfectly grave and fair use of the matter to which I refer. The circumstance to which I allude is, that in the third, fourth, and immediately following centuries – in the days of Cyprian, Cyril, Athanasius, and Chrysostom – when, as all agree, the mode of baptizing by immersion was the most prevalent method; there is no historical fact more perfectly established, than that whenever baptism was thus administered, the candidate, whether infant or adult, *male or female,* was *entirely divested of all clothing:* not merely of outer garments, but, I repeat, of *all clothing.* No exception was allowed in any case, even when the most timid and delicate female importunately desired it. This fact is established, not only by the most direct and unequivocal statements, and that by a number of writers, but also by the narration of a number of curious particulars connected with this practice.[2] Among the rest, we are told scenes of indecorum exhibited in the baptisteries of those days, which convinced the friends of religion that the practice ought to be discontinued, and it was finally laid aside. Perhaps it will be asked, whether this fact in the history of Christian baptism is adverted to for the purpose of reflecting odium, in a sinister and indirect manner, on the practice of immersion? I answer, by no means; but simply for the purpose of showing that in tracing the history of baptism by immersion, we have the *very same evidence* in favour of immersing *divested of all clothing,* that we have for

---

2. The zealous Baptist, Robert Robinson, bears, on this subject, the following testimony: "The primitive Christians baptized naked. Nothing is easier than to give proof of this by quotations from the authentic writings of the men who administered baptism, and who certainly knew in what way they themselves performed it. There is no ancient historical fact better authenticated than this. The evidence does not go on the evidence of the single word, *naked;* for then a reader might suspect allegory; but on facts reported, and many reasons assigned for the practice." *History of Baptism*, p. 85. He then quotes several examples dated in the fourth century.

immersing at all; that, so far as the history of the Church, subsequent to the apostolic age, informs us, these two practices must stand or fall together;[3] and that an appendage to baptism so revolting, so immoral, and so entirely inadmissible, plainly shows that those who practised it, must have been chargeable with a superstitious and extravagant adoption of a mere form, which, from its character, we are compelled to believe was a human invention, and took its rise in the rudeness of growing superstition, perhaps from a source still more impure and criminal.

Besides, if the principle for which our Baptist brethren contend, be correct; if the immersion of the whole body be essential to Christian baptism, and if the thing signified be the cleansing and purifying of the individual by an ablution which must of necessity extend to the whole person; it would really seem that performing this ceremony, divested of all clothing, is essential to its emblematic meaning. Who ever thought of covering the hands with gloves when they were about to be washed; or expected really to cleanse them through such a covering? No wonder, then, when the principle began to find a place in the Church, that the submersion of every part of the body in water; that the literal bathing of the whole person was essential both to the expressiveness and the validity of the emblematical transaction; no wonder, I say, that the obvious consequence should soon be admitted, that the whole body ought to be uncovered, as never fails to be the case, with any member of the body which we wish to be successfully cleansed by bathing. And we have no hesitation in saying,

---

3. The learned Wall speaks on the subject thus: "The ancient Christians, when they were baptized by immersion, were all baptized naked; whether they were men, women or children. The proofs of this, I shall omit, because it is a clear case. The English Antipædobaptists need not have made so great an outcry against Mr. Baxter for his saying that they baptized naked; for if they had, it would have been no more than the primitive Christians did. They thought it better represented the putting off the old man, and also the nakedness of Christ on the cross. Moreover, as baptism is a washing, they judged it should be the washing of the body, not of the clothes." Wall, Chapter XV. Part II.

that, if we fully adopted the general principle of our Baptist brethren in relation to this matter, we should no more think of subjecting the body to that process which must, in order to its validity, be strictly emblematical of a complete spiritual bathing, while covered with clothes, than we should think, in common life, of washing the hands or the feet, while carefully covered with the articles of dress with which they are commonly clothed. Whereas, if the principle of Pædobaptists on this subject be adopted, then the solemn application of water to that part of the body which is an epitome of the whole person, and which is always, as a matter of course, uncovered, is amply sufficient to answer every purpose both of emblem and of benefit.

Besides, let me appeal to our Baptist brethren, by asking, if they verily believe that the primitive and apostolic mode of administering baptism was by immersion, and that this immersion was performed in a state of entire nakedness; how can they dare, upon their principles, to depart, as to one iota from that mode? Let them not say, that they carefully retain the substance, the essential characters of the plan of immersion. Very true. This is our plea; and it accords very well with what we consider as the correct system; but in the mouth of a Baptist it is altogether inadmissible. The institute in question is a "positive" one; and, according to him, we must not depart one jot or tittle from the original plan.

These considerations, my friends, strike me as affording decisive evidence, that a mode of baptism, attended with so many real and formidable difficulties, cannot be of divine appointment; at any rate that it cannot be universally binding on the Church of God; and that laying so much stress upon the completeness of the submersion, is servility and superstition. We may say of this ordinance, as our Lord said of the Sabbath, *baptism was made for man, and not man for baptism.* Where a particular mode of complying with a religious observance would be, in many cases, "a yoke of bondage," and one, too, for which no divine warrant could be pleaded, it would surely argue the very slavery of superstition, to enforce that mode of the observance as essential to a regular standing in the visible family of Christ.

6. As a further objection to the doctrine of our Baptist brethren in relation to the mode of baptism, let us examine *some of the figurative language of Scripture which refers to this ordinance;* and especially, certain passages on which *they* are accustomed to place the greatest reliance for the support of their cause.

Perhaps no passages of Scripture have been more frequently and confidently pressed into the service of baptism by immersion than those which are found in Romans vi. 3, 4, and Colossians ii. 12. In the former we find the following: "Know ye not, that so many of us as were baptized into Jesus Christ, were baptized into his death? Therefore we are buried with him by baptism into death; that like as Christ was raised up from the dead by the glory of the Father, even so we also should walk in newness of life." Corresponding with this, in Colossians ii. 12, the following passage occurs: "Buried with him in baptism; wherein also ye are risen with him through the faith of the operation of God, who hath raised him from the dead."

Now, our Baptist brethren, believing and insisting that baptism and immersion ought to be considered, in all cases, as synonymous terms, take for granted that the expression, "buried with him in baptism," is intended to refer to the resemblance between the interment of a dead body, and its subsequent resurrection from beneath the surface of the earth; and the immersion of a baptized person entirely under the water, and raising him up again from beneath the surface of the fluid. In a word, our Baptist brethren assure us, that the design of the apostle in these passages is to say, that "the baptized person's communion with Christ in his death and burial, is represented by his being laid under the water; and his communion with him in his resurrection, by his being raised out of it." In this general interpretation of the figure many Pædobaptists have agreed; and have thus not a little confirmed the confidence of Antipædobaptists in their cause. I am persuaded, however, that a candid examination of the real import of the figurative language before us, will show that this confidence is entirely unfounded.

The apostle, in the preceding part of the Epistle to the Romans, had shown that Christians are justified by faith in the righteousness of Christ. He proceeds in the sixth chapter to obviate the objection, that this doctrine tends to licentiousness. "What shall we say, then? Shall we continue in sin that grace may abound? God forbid!" He rejects with abhorrence the odious thought. "How shall we that are dead to sin live any longer therein?" He then adverts to the significance of baptism, which, being the ordinance which seals our introduction into the family of Christ, may be considered as exhibiting both the first principles of Gospel truth, and the first elements of Christian character. "Know ye not, that so many of us as were baptized into Jesus Christ, were baptized into his death?" He then infers, that since baptism has so immediate a reference to the death of Christ, it must, by consequence, be connected also with His resurrection; and that, as in the former view, it teaches the regenerated the abandoning of the old life of sin; so, in the latter, it equally teaches them the pursuit and progress of the new life of righteousness. "Therefore we are buried with him by baptism into death; that like as Christ was raised up from the dead by the glory of the Father, even so we also should walk in newness of life."

The obvious design of the apostle is to illustrate the character and obligations of believers, from the circumstance, that they are, in a certain respect, conformed to Christ's *death:* that as He died *for* sin, so they are dead, or are under obligations to be dead, *to* sin; that is, they are holy, or are, by their profession, obliged to be holy. "So many of us as were baptized into Jesus Christ, were baptized into his death." And this is explained by what follows: "In that Christ died, he died unto sin [or on account of sin] once; but in that he liveth, he liveth unto God. Likewise reckon ye also yourselves to be dead indeed unto sin [or in respect to sin], but alive unto God through Jesus Christ." This is what was signified by baptism. And so believers were baptized *into Christ's death:* not that baptism was a symbol of *death,* or the state of the dead; for water, or washing in water, never was a symbol of this. But water, used in ceremonial, whether by washing or sprinkling, and afterwards in Christian baptism, always signified the *fact,* or the acknowledged *necessity* of *purification.* Now being *dead,* or in a state of *death to sin,* is the same thing as to be *spiritually purified,* or made *holy.* And this is the very thing that *baptism,* coming in the place of absolutions under the former economy, is exactly adapted to signify. Or, to say all in a word, water used in baptism is a sign of that moral purification of believers, which the apostle means to express by their being *crucified, dead* and conformed to Christ's death." Their being *dead* in conformity with Christ, is the expression which contains the metaphor. And baptism, as an appointed token or *symbol,* denotes what is signified by the metaphor, not the metaphor itself."[4] The sum of the apostle's illustrations, then, so far as the point before us is concerned, is simply this: That in baptism, as a rite emblematical of *moral purification,* Christians profess to be baptized *into the death of Christ,* as well as *into* (or into the hope of) *His resurrection;* that they are *dead* and *buried* in respect to sin, that is, in a moral and spiritual sense; so that every Christian can say, with Paul: "I am crucified with Christ; I have been made conformable to his death; being dead indeed to sin, and alive to God by Jesus Christ."

But besides all this, which is sufficient of itself to show how little reliance is to be placed on the gloss of this passage adopted by our Baptist brethren – the burial of Christ was by no means such as the friends of this exposition commonly suppose. The body of our Saviour was never buried in the manner in which we are accustomed to inter human corpses, that is by letting it down into the bosom of the earth, and covering it with earth. It was placed in a tomb hewn out of a rock; not a tomb sunk in the

---

4. See Dr. Woods' *Lectures on Infant Baptism,* p. 18, 189. See this interpretation of Rom. vi. 3, 4, and the corresponding passage in Colossians ii. 12, well illustrated in the *Essay on Baptism,* by Greville Ewing, D. D. of Glasgow, and also in a *Dissertation on infant Baptism,* by Ralph Wardlaw, D. D. of Glasgow; and still more recently, by Professor Stuart, in the *Biblical Repository,* p. 327. 332.

earth, but hollowed out of a rock, above ground, and containing separate cells for the reception of bodies, "as the manner of the Jews was to bury." Even supposing, then, that it were yielded to our Baptist brethren that the design of the apostle is to teach the *mode* of baptism, by comparing it to the burial of Christ, it would by no means serve their purpose. There was not in fact any such subterranean immersion, if the expression may be allowed, as they imagine. The body of the Saviour was evidently laid in a stone cell, above ground, in which no earth came in contact with it, and in which, when the stone which closed up the door was taken away, the body was distinctly visible. In short, the burial of Christ no more resembled the modern interment of a dead body among us, than the depositing such a body, for a time, in an apartment in the basement story of a dwelling house, the floor of which was either not sunk below the surface of the earth at all, or, if any, not more than a few inches; admitting of free ingress and egress as a common inhabited room. The figure in question, then, does not serve the turn of our Baptist brethren thus affording another proof that nothing more was intended by its use, than to set forth that, by being *baptized into the death of Christ,* we profess to be *dead* and *buried in respect to sin,* without any reference whatever to the *mode* in which either the burial or the baptism might be performed.

Accordingly, in the verse immediately preceding that before commented on, in the second Epistle to the Colossians, the following passage occurs, evidently intended to teach the same lesson: "In whom also ye are circumcised with the circumcision made without hands, in putting off the body of the sins of the flesh, by the circumcision of Christ." And in the verse immediately following that in which the burial of Christ is alluded to, the figure of circumcision as an emblem of spiritual cleansing, is still pursued: "And you being dead in your sins, and the uncircumcision of your flesh, hath he quickened together with him, having forgiven you all trespasses." Here, it is plain, the same general idea is meant to be conveyed, as in the reference to baptism, which has come in the room of circumcision. In both the putting away sin; the "putting off the sins of the flesh," is emblematically represented and sealed: as a man dead and buried is cut off from all temporal connections and indulgences; so the baptized man is really, or at least by profession, dead to sin, and in this way made conformable to the death of Christ, in its great design and efficacy, which are to purify to himself a peculiar people, dead to the world, dead to carnal ambition, and secluded from every unhallowed practice.

Another signal example of the figurative language of Scripture applied to baptism, occurs in 1 Corinthians, x. 1, 2. "Moreover, brethren, I would not that ye should be ignorant, how that all our fathers were under the cloud, and all passed through the sea; and were all baptized unto Moses in the cloud and in the sea." Now, when we turn to the narrative given by Moses, in the fourteenth chapter of Exodus, we find that the Red Sea, through which the Israelites passed, was divided before them; that the waters stood up like a wall on each side; and that they passed through ON DRY GROUND. We are also informed, that the cloud by which their line of march was divinely directed, did not even fall upon them in the form of a shower, much less submerge them; but that it alternately went *behind* them and *before* them; now hanging in their rear, for the purpose of concealing them from their enemies; and then preceding them in their course, presenting a face of splendour to them, and a face of darkness to their pursuers. In all this, there was evidently nothing like immersion. The utmost that could have happened, in consistency with the inspired narrative, was their being sprinkled by the spray of the sea, or by drops from the miraculous cloud, when it passed over their heads.

The last passage of the class under consideration to which I shall advert, is that found in the first Epistle of Peter, iii. 20, 21: "The long-suffering of God waited in the days of Noah, while the ark was preparing, wherein few, that is eight souls, were saved by water. The like figure whereunto even baptism doth also now save us (not the putting away of the filth of the flesh, but the answer of a good conscience toward God) by the resurrection of Jesus Christ." The principle implied in this passage is plain; and it affords not the smallest countenance to the doctrine of our Baptist brethren. Every one sees, that in the case of Noah and his family, and of all the animals preserved with them in the ark, there was no immersion in the waters of the flood. Nay, this was the very evil from which the ark preserved them. Of course, whatever else the passage may prove, it is impossible that it should be legitimately considered as favouring baptism by plunging the whole body under water.

7. Further; that immersion is not necessary in baptism; and that to insist upon it, as indispensable, is superstition, appears from the indisputable fact, that *both the significance and the effect of baptism are to be considered as depending, not on the physical influence of water, or upon the quantity of it employed, but on its symbolical meaning, and on the blessing of God upon its application as a symbol.* There has always been a tendency in human nature to lay more stress than the Bible warrants upon outward forms; and to imagine that external rites have a virtue inherent in themselves, by which their recipients are of course savingly benefited. It is generally granted by enlightened Protestants to be one of the mischievous errors of Popery, that baptism, and the other appointed rites of our religion, when administered by authorized hands, have an inherent efficacy; a sort of self-operating power on those to whom they are administered. This we consider as a superstitious and dangerous error. We believe that no external ordinance has any power in itself; but that its power to benefit those who receive it depends altogether upon the influence of the Holy Spirit of God making it effectual; and that this influence may accompany or follow the ordinance, whatever may be the outward form of its administration. If, indeed, we had reason to believe that the benefit of baptism was caused by the physical influence of water on any or every part of the body, and depended upon that influence – if the least intimation of this kind were given us, either by the Word of God, or the nature of the case – it would be wise to insist on a rigorous adherence to that form. But as the benefit of the ordinance has no connection, so far as we know, with the operation of water on the animal frame;

but is the result, solely, of a divine blessing on a prescribed and striking emblem; and as the Word of God has no where informed us of the precise mode in which that emblem shall be applied – we infer that the divine blessing may attend upon any mode of applying it. The language of our blessed Saviour, on a memorable occasion, is full of instruction on this subject. In order to give His disciples a striking lesson both of humility and purity, He condescended, on a certain evening, when they were assembled under solemn circumstances, to *wash their feet*. Simon Peter, when his Master came to him, like too many at the present day, misunderstanding the nature and significance of the symbolical action, at first strongly objected, and said, "Thou shalt never wash my feet." Jesus answered, "If I wash thee not, thou hast no part in me." To which Peter, in the fulness of his fervent zeal, replied, "Lord, not my feet only, but also my hands and my head." Jesus, however, meaning to convey the idea that the whole action was symbolical, and that the application of water to any part of the body was abundantly sufficient, rejoins to Peter, "He that is washed needeth not save to wash his feet, but is clean every whit:" as much as to say, "It is not the *physical ablution,* but the *symbolical meaning,* to which I now wish to call your attention; and for this purpose the application of water to the feet only, carries with it all the fulness of meaning, and all the richness of benefit, that could have resulted from the most plentiful application of it to the whole frame."

8. Another, and in my view, conclusive reason for believing that our Baptist brethren are in error, in insisting that no baptism unless by immersion is valid, is, *that the native tendency of this doctrine is to superstition and abuse.* The tendency here alleged has been often observed and lamented by serious people, as likely to be connected with a false hope, and to destroy the souls of multitudes. Facts in support of this remark have fallen under my own painful observation. I have known many Baptists, who appeared to feel as if there was some *inherent efficacy* in being "buried under the water," and that those who submitted to that "self-denying" rite, were, of course, real Christians. They have

evidently appeared to think that *that* was the *great step* in religion; and that, having taken it, all was secure. Now, I contend, that this is the *natural tendency* of the Baptist doctrine; that their laying so much stress upon "going under the water," and holding it up, with unceasing zeal, to the popular view as the great, distinguishing, and indispensable badge of discipleship, is, unavoidably, adapted to betray "unwary souls" into a delusive confidence. There is no disposition in depraved human nature more deeply inwrought, or more incessantly operative, than the disposition to rely upon something done by us for securing the divine favour. It is this disposition which has led to all that enormous mass of superstitious observances which distinguishes the Papal system, and which we have every reason to believe is built upon by millions as the foundation of hope, instead of Christ. Whenever, therefore, any external rite becomes the grand distinction of a sect, and the object of something approaching to sectarian idolatry, we may be sure there exists not only the danger, but the actual commencement, to some extent, of that superstitious reliance, which he who has not learned to fear, "knows nothing of the human heart yet as he ought to know."

That this suggestion has something more than mere fancy on which to rest, is evident from facts of recent and most mournful occurrence. A large and daily increasing sect has arisen, within a few years, in the bosom of the Baptist denomination, which maintains the delusive and destructive doctrine that baptism is regeneration; that no man can be regenerated who is not immersed; and that all, without exception, who have a historical faith, and are immersed, are, of course, in a state of salvation. This pernicious heresy, so contrary to the plainest principles and facts of the Word of God, and so manifestly adapted to destroy the souls of all who believe it, has been propagated to a melancholy extent, by a plausible, reckless, and impious demagogue, and is supposed to embrace one half of the Baptist body in the western country, besides many in the east. In short, the Baptist churches, in large districts of country, are so rent in pieces, and deluded by the miserable impostor referred to, that their prospects, for many years to come, are not only gloomy, but, without a special interposition of the King of Zion in their favour, altogether desperate.

Now I maintain that this wretched delusion is by no means an unnatural result of the doctrine and practice of our Baptist brethren, in regard to the baptismal rite. Multitudes of them, I know, reject and abhor the heresy in question as much as any of us. But have they duly considered, that it seems naturally to have grown out of their own theory and practice in regard to baptism; their attaching such a disproportioned importance to the mode of administering that ordinance; often, very often, directing the attention of the people more to the river than the cross; excluding all from Christian communion, however pious, who have not been immersed; and making representations which, whether so intended or not, naturally lead the weak and the uninformed to consider immersion as a kind of talisman, always connected with a saving blessing? This, I sincerely believe, is the native tendency of the doctrine of our Baptist brethren, although *they,* I am equally confident, neither perceive nor admit this to be the case. If pious Christians who have not been immersed, cannot be admitted to communion in the Church below, there would seem to be still more reason for excluding them from the purer Church above. And so far as this principle is received and cherished, though far from being alike mischievous in all cases, it can scarcely fail of predisposing many minds in favour of that awful delusion, by which we have reason to believe that not a few, under its higher workings, have been blinded, betrayed, and lost.

9. Finally; that immersion cannot be considered, to say the least, as *essential* to a valid baptism, is plain *from the history of this ordinance.*

It is not denied that, for the first few centuries after Christ, the most common mode of administering baptism was by immersion. But it is maintained, that affusion and sprinkling were also practised, and when used, were considered as perfectly valid and sufficient. Of this the proof is so complete and indubitable, that no one really acquainted with the early history of the Church, will think, for a moment, of calling it in question. The learned Wall, whose *History of Infant Baptism* is generally considered, by competent judges, as one of the most profound and faithful works extant on the subject before us; after showing conclusively that Pædobaptists ought not to refuse the admission that baptism by dipping was the most prevalent mode, even in the western Church, for a number of centuries after Christ; goes on to remark that, on the other hand, the Antipædobaptists will be quite as unfair in their turn, if they do not grant, that in cases of sickness, weakliness, haste, want of a sufficient quantity of water, or any such extraordinary occasion, baptism by the affusion of water on the face, was, by the ancients, counted sufficient baptism. Of the testimony which he offers in support of this statement, a specimen will be presented.[5]

Eusebius states, on the authority of preceding writers, that Novatian being sick, and near death, as was supposed, was baptized on his bed by affusion (Book 6, chapter 43). He, however, recovered, and was afterwards ordained to the work of the ministry. And although some questioned, whether a man who had been brought to make a profession of religion only on a sick bed, and when he considered himself as about to die, ought to be made a minister; yet this doubt arose, we are assured, not from any apprehension that the baptism itself was incomplete; but on the principle, that he who came to the faith not voluntarily, but from necessity, ought not to be made a priest, unless his subsequent diligence and faith should be distinguished and highly commendable.

Of the character of Cyprian, who flourished in the former part of the third century, enough has been said in a preceding discourse. A certain Magnus, a country minister, consulted him on the question, whether those who had been introduced into the Christian Church, by baptism, on their sick beds, and, of course, by affusion, or sprinkling, ought to be baptized again, if they re-

---

5. Wall, Part II. chapter ix. p. 352, &c.

covered? Cyprian's answer to this question is as follows:

"You inquire, my dear son, what I think of such as attain grace in time of sickness and infirmity: whether they are to be accounted lawful Christians, because they have not been *washed all over* with the water of salvation, but have only had some of it *poured on them*. In which matter I would use so much modesty and humility, as not to prescribe so positively, but that every one should enjoy the freedom of his own thought, and do as he thinks best. I do, however, according to the best of my mean capacity, judge thus: That the divine favours can in no wise be mutilated or weakened, so that any thing less than the whole of them is conveyed, where the benefit of them is received with a full and complete faith, on the part both of the giver and receiver. For, in the sacrament of salvation, the contagion of sin is not washed off in the same manner as the filth of the body is in a carnal and secular bath. It is entirely in a different way that the heart of a believer – it is after another fashion that the mind of man is by faith cleansed. In the sacraments of salvation, through the indulgence of God, when necessity compels, the shortest way of transacting divine matters, conveys the whole benefit to those who believe. Nor let any be moved by the fact, that the sick, when they are baptized, are only perfused or sprinkled, since the Scripture says, by the prophet Ezekiel, "I will sprinkle clean water upon you, and ye shall be clean; from all your filthiness and from all your idols will I cleanse you; a new heart also will I give you, and a new spirit will I put within you" (chapter xxxvi. 25. 36). It is also said in the book of Numbers, "And the man which shall be unclean until the evening, shall be purified on the third day, and on the seventh day, and he shall be clean. But if he shall not be purified on the third day, and on the seventh day, he shall not be clean, and that soul shall be cut off from Israel, because the water of aspersion hath not been sprinkled upon him" (chap. xix). And again, the Lord spake unto Moses, in the book of Numbers, "Take the Levites from among the children of Israel, and cleanse them; and thus shalt thou do unto them to cleanse them; sprinkle water of purifying upon them" (chap. viii). And again, "the water

of aspersion is purification." From which it appears that sprinkling is sufficient instead of immersion; and whensoever it is
done, if there be a sound faith, on the part both of the giver and
receiver, it is perfect and complete.

From these passages, as well as from a number of others,
which might be quoted, found in the works of Cyprian, it is evident, that, in a little more than one hundred and fifty years from
the death of the last apostle, cases of baptism by perfusion or
sprinkling had notoriously, and in repeated instances, occurred;
that such examples were found among the heretics, as well as in
the orthodox Church; that a man so learned and pious as the venerable Cyprian, was decisively of the opinion that they were to be
justified; and, finally, that he considered this as a point concerning
which Christians were at liberty to entertain their own opinion,
and to do as they judged best. Plainly implying that he did not
consider it at all as an essential matter.

Origen was contemporary with Cyprian. He wrote in the
Greek language. It was his vernacular tongue; and he was, probably, the most learned man of the century in which he lived. This
venerable Christian father, commmenting on 1 Kings, xviii. 33, in
which we read of Elijah's ordering water to be *poured* on the
burnt sacrifice, tells us that he *baptized* the wood on the altar.
Was not Origen a good judge of the meaning of a Greek word?
Can we imagine that he would have used the word *baptize* in this
sense, if he had regarded immersion as its exclusive meaning?

When Laurentius, a Roman deacon, about the middle of
the third century, was brought to the stake to suffer martyrdom,
a soldier who had been employed to be one of his executioners,
professed to be converted, and requested baptism from the hands
of him whom he had been engaged to assist in burning. For this
purpose, a *pitcher of water* was brought, and the soldier baptized
at the place of execution.[6] In circumstances so solemn as these,
surely no conscientious man would have sported with a divine or-

---

6. Walfridius Strabo, *De Rebus Ecciesiast*, as quoted by Wall.

dinance, or subjected it to any essential mutilation. It was, doubt-less, deemed a sufficient mode of administering baptism.

Gennadius, a distinguished ecclesiastic of Marseilles, in the fifth century, speaks of baptism as administered in the French Church indifferently, by either immersion or affusion, or sprin-kling. For having said, "We believe the way of salvation to be open only to baptized persons"; he adds, "except only in the case of martyrdom, in which all the sacraments of baptism are com-pleted." Then, to show how martyrdom has all in it that baptism has, he says, "The person to be baptized, owns his faith before the priest; and when the interrogatories are put to him, makes his answer. The same does a martyr before the heathen judge. He also owns his faith; and when the question is put to him, makes answer. The one, after his confession, is either wetted with the water, or else plunged into it; and the other, is either wetted with his own blood, or plunged into the *fire.*" This language plainly evinces that, in the time of Gennadius, both modes of baptism were in use and deemed equally valid.

Thomas Aquinas, and Bonaventura, are well known as two learned ecclesiastics of the twelfth century. In their time it is evident that both plunging and affusion were used in the churches of Italy, in the administration of baptism. Aquinas, in writing on the subject, expresses himself this: "Baptism may be given not only by immersion, but also by affusion of water, or by sprinkling with it. But it is the safer way to baptize by immersion, because that is the most common custom." On the other hand, his con-temporary, Bonaventura, observes, "The way of affusion in bap-tism was *probably used by the apostles,* and was, in his time, used in the churches of France, and some others;" but remarks, "The method of dipping into the water is the more common, and therefore the fitter and safer."

The Synod of Angiers, A.D. 1275, speaks of *dipping* and *pouring* as indifferently used; and blames some ignorant priests, because they *dipped,* or *poured on water,* but *once* and at the same time declaring that the general custom of the Church was to dip, or to pour on water *three times.* The Synod of Langres, A.D.

1404, speaks of pouring or perfusion only. "Let the priest make three pourings or sprinklings of water on the *infant's* head," &c. The Council of Cologne, in 1536, evidently intimate that both modes were constantly practised. Their language is, "The child is thrice either *dipped,* or *wetted* with water." Fifteen years afterwards, in the Agenda of the Church of Mentz, published by Sebastian, there is found the following direction: "Then let the priest take the *child* on his left arm, and holding him over the font, let him, with his right hand, three several times, take water out of the font, and pour it on the child's head, so that the water may wet its head and shoulders." Then they give a note to this purpose; that immersion, once or thrice, or pouring of water may be used, and have been used, in the Church; that this variety does not alter the nature of baptism; and that a man would do ill to break the custom of the Church for either of them. But they add, that it is better, if the Church will allow, to use *pouring on* of water. "For suppose," say they, "the priest be old and feeble, or have the palsy in his hands; or the weather be very cold; or the *child* be very infirm; or too big to be dipped in the font; then it is much fitter to use affusion of the water." Then they bring the instance of the apostles baptizing *three thousand* at a time; and the instance of Laurentius, the Roman deacon, before spoken of – and add, "That, therefore, there may not be one way for the sick, and another for the healthy; one for children, and another for bigger persons; it is better that the administrator of this sacrament do observe the safest way, which is, to pour water thrice; unless the custom be to the contrary."[7]

One more historical record, which, though apparently inconsiderable in itself, is, in my view, decisive, shall close the present list of testimonies. It is one referred to in a former discourse, when speaking of *infant* baptism. I mean the undoubted fact, that the Waldenses, those far-famed and devoted witnesses of the truth, who maintained, during the darkness and desolation

---

7. Wall, Part II, chapter ix. p. 360, 361.

of the Papacy, "the testimony of Jesus," very soon after the Reformation opened, approached, with the most cordial friendliness, the Reformed churches of Geneva and France; recognised them as sisters in the Lord; received ministers from them and maintained with them the most affectionate communion. Now it is certain that, at that time, in the churches of both Geneva and France, the baptism of *infants,* and the administration of the ordinance by *sprinkling,* were in constant use. On such an incontestible fact, the argument is this: The Waldenses either baptized by *sprinkling* or by *immersion.* If by *sprinkling,* an important testimony is gained in favour of that mode, from ecclesiastical history. If by *immersion,* they plainly laid no such stress upon the mode as our Baptist brethren now do; since they were willing to commune with, and to receive ministers from, churches which were in the habit of using sprinkling only. In my view, as I said, this argument is decisive. We *know* that the Waldenses habitually baptized *infants;* but in what *mode* they administered the ordinance is not quite so certain. But one thing is unquestionable; and that is, that those pious witnesses for Christ, even if they did immerse, did not consider the mode as *essential,* but were ready to hold the most unreserved communion with those who practised aspersion.

These testimonies, and many more to the same purpose, which might be presented if it were necessary, must, it appears to me, satisfy every impartial mind, that, from the days of the apostles down to the Reformation, affusion and sprinkling in baptism, as well as immersion, have been in constant use; that some of the gravest and most sober-minded writers have firmly defended the two former, as well as the latter; that the strong arguments in favour of affusion or sprinkling, as the preferable mode, have been, in all ages, distinctly appreciated; and that it has ever been considered as a part of *Christian liberty* to use *either* mode, as may be conscientiously preferred.

Suffer me now to close this discussion by presenting two or three practical inferences from the view which has been given of this latter part of the subject. And,

1. If our statement of evidence as to the mode of baptism be correct, then the conduct of our Baptist brethren, in not only denying to the infant seed of believers all right to membership in the Church, but also making immersion *indispensable* to a valid baptism, are chargeable with taking ground which is plainly unscriptural, and with dividing the Body of Christ, for a mere uncommanded circumstance; a circumstance in regard to which all reasoning, and all history are, on the whole, against them. We do not deny that the baptisms of these brethren are valid; but we do deny that they rest upon any more solid ground than ours; and we are persuaded that, without the least authority, they lay on the recipients of baptism "a yoke of bondage," which has no warrant from the Word of God; and which the whole genius of the Gospel forbids. Surely, if the inspired writers had regarded immersion in the same light with our Baptist brethren, we should have had some explicit statements on this subject in the instructions given to the churches in the infancy of their New Testament course. And, surely, the attempt to lay burdens which the Spirit of God has no where authorized, is to incur the guilt imputed to those who "add to" the things which are contained in the Book of Life. On this subject I feel that it is no longer our duty to content ourselves with standing on the defensive. Our opponents in this controversy, I verily believe, are chargeable with "teaching for doctrines the commandments of men;" and, of course, I consider them as equally sinning against the Head of the Church, and against "the generation of the righteous."

2. These things being so, we may see how the conduct of *some* of our Baptist brethren, in particular states of the Church, ought to be regarded by the friends of Zion. The conduct to which I refer is, their having so often intruded into churches in which some religious attention has existed, and in which scarcely a family of their own denomination was to be found; and when the minds of many individuals were anxious respecting their eternal interest, immediately broaching the controversy respecting infant baptism, and immersion, and distressing the consciences of serious inquirers – not with the great and momentous question,

"what they shall do to be saved?" – but before their minds are at all settled as to their personal hope in Christ, or their fitness for any sacramental seal, perplexing them with the controversy about an external rite, which they themselves grant is not essential to salvation. I have personally known such proceedings to occur, with a frequency as wonderful as it was revolting; and with an obtrusive zeal worthy of a better cause. Young and timid consciences have been distressed, if not with the direct assertion, at least by the artful insinuation, that their particular mode of baptism was all in all; that there could be no safe Christianity without it. *The river, the river,* really seemed, by some, to be placed in the room of the *Saviour!*

There is something in all this so deeply offensive to every enlightened and judicious Christian; which involves so much meanness; and which manifests so much more concern for the enlargement of a sect, than the salvation of souls, that it is difficult to speak of it in terms of as strong reprobation as it deserves, without infringing on the limits of Christian decorum and respectfulness. It is conduct of which no candid and generous mind, actuated by the Spirit of Christ, will ever be guilty. And, I am happy to add: it is conduct in which many belonging to the denomination to which I allude, have souls too enlarged and elevated to allow themselves to indulge.

3. Once more; let us all be careful, my Christian friends, as a practical deduction from what has been said, to forbear "returning evil for evil," on this, or any other point of ecclesiastical controversy. However other denominations may treat *us,* let us never be chargeable with treating *them* in an unchristian manner. We are conscientiously compelled to differ from our Baptist brethren. We believe them to be in error; in important and highly mischievous error. But what then? They are still brethren in Christ. Let us, therefore, love them, and, however they may treat us, treat them with fraternal respectfulness, and seek their welfare. Let us never indulge a spirit of unhallowed proselytism. Let us never employ any other weapons against them than those of candid argument, and fervent prayer. Instead of "doting about

questions, and strifes of words, whereof come envy, railings, evil surmisings, and corrupt disputings;" let us follow after patience, forbearance and charity; over remembering that all who really belong to Christ, however they may differ in externals, are "one body in Him, and members one of another." May we all be deeply imbued with the spirit which ought to flow from this precious truth; and may all that we do be done with charity! Amen!

APPENDIX ONE

Giving a Name in Baptism

In administering the rite of *circumcision,* it was customary to give a *name* to the child. This is evident from the circumstances attending the circumcision of John the Baptist, as related in the Gospel according to Luke, i. 59-64; and also those attending the circumcision of our blessed Saviour, as found recorded in the next chapter of the same Gospel. The same practice probably existed, from the earliest period of the New Testament Church, in the administration of *baptism.* It makes, however, no *necessary,* or even *important,* part of the rite. A baptism administered *without a name,* would, of course, be just as valid as if one were announced. And there is nothing in the essential nature of the case, which would forbid a name given to a child in baptism being *reconsidered* and *altered* afterwards. Yet, inasmuch as a child, when baptized, is announced to the church as a new member, subject to its maternal watch and care, it ought, in common, for obvious reasons, to be introduced and known under some name, so that each child may be distinguished, and may receive its appropriate treatment. To introduce a *nameless* member into any society, would be both unreasonable and inconvenient. Moreover, it is of great consequence, both to civil and religious society, that the birth and baptism of every child be *recorded* in regular church books. The formation of this record requires, it is evident, the use of a *name;* and after the name is adopted and recorded in this public register, it is plain that frequent alterations of the name, and tampering, in a corresponding manner, with the public register, would lead to endless confusion and mischief. Thus we are conducted, by a very obvious train of reasoning, to the conclusion that the name announced in baptism, ought, in general, to be carefully retained, without subtraction or addition. Sometimes, indeed, the civil law requires such registers to be made and preserved, in regard to every birth and baptism. Where this is the case, there is, evidently, an additional reason for adhering strictly to the name announced in baptism, recorded in the appropriate register, and thus brought under official notice, and recorded as the property of the State. See a number of curious questions proposed and resolved, concerning the names imposed in baptism, in the *Politicæ Eclesiasticæ* of the learned Gisbertus Voetius, Tom. I. p. 714-724.

APPENDIX TWO

Baptismal Regeneration

This unscriptural and pernicious doctrine is not confined to the *Roman Catholics,* in whose system it may without impropriety be said to be indigenous; but is also frequently found in the pulpits and the manuals of some *Protestants,* in the midst of whose general principles it ought to be regarded as a poisonous exotic.

I. The doctrine referred to, as held by some Protestants, in its most objectionable form, appears to be this: that the spiritual change which the Scriptures designate by the term *regeneration,* is always attendant upon, and effected by, the rite of baptism, when duly administered; that, on the one hand, every person, infant or adult, who has been baptized by an authorized minister, is a regenerated person; and that, on the other, every person who has not been baptized, however deep or mature his penitence and faith, is still unregenerate. In short, the position is, that the inward grace of regeneration *always* accompanies the outward sign of baptism; that they are inseparable; that the one cannot exist without the other; that he who has been thus regenerated, if he die without falling from grace, is certainly saved; that baptism is essential to salvation; and that to call by the name of regeneration any moral change, from the love of sin to the love of holiness, which takes place either *before* or *after* baptism, is unscriptural and absurd. This, as I understand them, is the doctrine maintained by Bishop Tomline, Bishop Marsh, Bishop Mant, and a number of other writers, of equal conspicuity, in the Church of England, and by not a few divines of the Protestant Episcopal Church in our own country.

This doctrine, I apprehend, is contrary to Scripture; contrary to experience; contrary to the declared opinion of the most wise, pious, and venerated divines even of the Episcopal denomination; and adapted to generate the most dangerous errors with regard to Christian character, and the Gospel plan of salvation.

1. It is contrary to *Scripture*. Without regeneration, the Scriptures declare, it is impossible to enter into the kingdom of heaven. But the penitent malefactor on the cross undoubtedly entered into the kingdom of heaven, if we are to credit our Lord's express declaration. Yet this penitent, believing malefactor was never baptized, therefore he was regenerated without baptism; and, of course, regeneration and baptism are not inseparably connected. Again; Simon Magus received the outward and visible ordinance of baptism, with unquestionable regularity, by an authorized administrator; yet who will venture to say, that he received the "inward and invisible grace" signified and represented in that ordinance? He was evidently from the beginning a hypocrite, and remained, after baptism, as before "in the gall of bitterness and in the bond of iniquity." Therefore the outward and sensible sign, and the inward and invisible grace are not in *all cases,* or *necessarily,* connected. Again; it is evident that the apostle Paul, Lydia, the Ethiopian Eunuch, the Philippian Jailor, &c. "believed with the heart," and were, consequently, brought into a state of acceptance with God *before* they were baptized. But we are told that as many as believe have been "born of God," and made the "sons of God" (John i. 12, 13). Of course, regeneration *may* take place, in the case of *adults, ought* to take place, and in these cases, *did* take place, *before* baptism; and, consequently, is not *the same thing* with baptism, or inseparably connected with that rite. Once more; we are assured in Scripture, that "he who is born of God, or regenerated, doth not commit sin [that is, deliberately or habitually], for his seed remaineth in him, and he cannot sin, because he is born of God;" and farther, that

"every one that loveth is born of God and knoweth God;" and that "whosoever believeth that Jesus is the Christ, is born of God." But can it be said that this character belongs to all who are baptized? Or, that none who are unbaptized manifest that they possess it? Surely no one in his senses will venture to make the assertion. Therefore a man may be "born of God" before he is baptized, and, consequently, the administration of the outward ordinance, and that work of the Holy Spirit, called in the Word of God regeneration, are not always connected.

2. The doctrine before us is as contrary to *experience* as it is to Scripture. "It is asserted," says an eminent divine of the Church of England, now living – "It is asserted, that the spiritual change of heart called regeneration invariably takes place in the precise article of baptism. If this assertion be well founded, the spiritual change in question will invariably take place in every adult at the identical moment when he is baptized; that is to say, at the very instant when the hand of the priest brings his body in contact with the baptismal water; at that precise instant, his understanding begins to be illuminated, his will to be reformed, and his affections to be purified. Hitherto he has walked in darkness; but now, to use the scriptural phrase, he has passed from darkness to light. Hitherto he has been wrapped in a death-like sleep of trespasses and sins; but now he awakes, and rises from the dead, Christ himself giving him life. Hitherto he has been a chaos of vice, and ignorance, and spiritual confusion; the natural man receiving not the things of the Spirit of God, for they are foolishness unto him: but *now* he is created after God in righteousness and true holiness; being in Christ he is a 'new creature;' having become spiritual, the things of the Spirit of God are no longer foolishness to him; he knows them because they are spiritually discerned. Such are the emphatic terms in which regeneration is described by the inspired writers. What we have to do, therefore, I apprehend, is forthwith to inquire, whether every baptized adult, without a single exception, is invariably found to declare, that, in the precise article of baptism, his soul experienced a change analogous to that which is so unequivocally set forth in the above-

mentioned texts of Scripture."[1] We need not dwell long on the inquiry. The fact is notoriously not so. Nor does it diminish the difficulty, in admitting the doctrine of baptismal regeneration, to say, as the Arminian advocates of this doctrine invariably do say, that those who are once regenerated may fall from grace, and manifest a most unhallowed temper. This is not the question. The question is, does experience evince that every subject of baptism, who has reached an age capable of manifesting the Christian character, does, *at the moment of receiving the baptismal water,* show that he is the subject of that regenerating power of the Holy Spirit, by which "old things are passed away, and all things become new in the Lord"? No one who has a particle of intelligence or candour can imagine that any such fact exists but if it do not, then the doctrine under consideration falls of course.

3. The doctrine of baptismal regeneration is contrary to the declared opinion of the most pious, judicious, and venerable Protestant divines, including those of the very highest authority in the Church of England. Nothing can be more certain than that the mass of the English reformers distinctly taught that baptism is a *sign* only of regeneration, and that the thing signified might or might not accompany the administration of the outward ordinance, according as it was received worthily or otherwise. In support of this assertion, the most explicit quotations might be presented from the writings of those distinguished martyrs and prelates, Cranmer, Latimer, Ridley, and Hooper; and after them from the writings of the eminent bishops, Jewell, Davenant, Hall, Usher, Reynolds, Leighton, Hopkins, Tillotson, Beveridge, Burnet, Seeker, and a host of other divines of the English Church, of whose elevated character it would be little less than an insult to any intelligent reader to attempt to offer testimony. All these men declare in the most solemn manner, against the doctrine of baptismal regeneration, in the sense which we are now considering. Indeed, I cannot call to mind a single writer of that church, from

---

1. Faber's *Sermons*, Vol. I, p. 145, 146.

the time of Archbishop Cranmer to the present hour, who had the least claim to the character of an *evangelical* man, who did not repudiate the doctrine which I am now opposing; and not a few of them denounce it as *Popish,* and adapted to subvert the whole system of vital and spiritual religion.

4. The last argument which I shall urge against the doctrine of baptismal regeneration, is, that is it adapted to generate the most *fatal errors* with regard to the Gospel plan of salvation. So far as this doctrine is believed, its native tendency is, to beget a superstitious and unwarranted reliance on an external ordinance; to lower our estimate of that inward spiritual sanctification which constitutes the essence of the Christian character; in fact, to supersede the necessity of that spiritual change of heart, of which the Scriptures speak so much, and for which the most holy and eminent servants of Christ have, in all ages, contended. The truth is, the doctrine now under consideration is the very same, in substance, with the doctrine of the *opus operatuni* of the *Papists,* which all evangelical Protestants have been opposing for more than three hundred years, as a mischievous delusion. Accordingly, the Popish character and fatal tendency of this error have been unreservedly acknowledged by many bishops, and other pious divines of the Church of England, as well as by many of the same denomination in this country.

Further; if regeneration, which is the commencement of holiness in the soul, is always communicated in baptism, then it follows, – as, indeed, those who entertain this doctrine distinctly avow, – that baptism invariably places its subject in a state of salvation; so that every baptized person who dies immediately after the administration of this sacrament, is infallibly sure of entering the kingdom of heaven. If this doctrine were fully believed, would not every thinking, anxious parent refrain from having his child baptized in infancy, and reserve the ordinance for an hour of extremity, such as the approach of death, that it might serve as an unfailing passport to glory? Would it not be wise in every adult who may be brought to a knowledge of the Saviour, from Paganism, or from the world, to put off his baptism to the last hour of his life, that he might be sure of departing in safety? This is well known to have been one of the actual corruptions of the fourth century, growing out of the very error which I am now opposing. "It was the custom of many," says Dr. Mosheim, in that century, to put off their baptism till the last hour; that thus immediately after receiving by this rite the remission of their sins, they might ascend pure and spotless to the mansions of life and immortality." This is no far-fetched or strange conceit. It is the native fruit of the doctrine before us. Nay, if we suppose this pernicious theory to take full possession of the mind, would it not be natural that a tender parent should anxiously desire his child to *die* immediately after baptism; or even, in a desperate case, to *compass its death,* as infallibly for its eternal benefit? And, on the same principle, might we not pray for the death of every adult, immediately after he had received baptism, believing that *then* "to die would certainly be gain"? In fine, I see not, if the doctrine be true, that a regenerating and saving efficacy attends every regular baptism – I see not how we can avoid the conclusion, that every Pagan, whether child or adult, that can be seized by force, and, however thoughtless, reluctant or profane, made to submit to the rite of baptism, is thereby infallibly made "a child of God, and an inheritor of the kingdom of heaven"!

These consequences, which appear to me demonstrably to flow from the theory in question, afford sufficient evidence that it is an unscriptural and pernicious error, even if no other means of refutation could be found.

It is not forgotten that language which seems, at first view, to countenance the doctrine which I am opposing, is found in some of the *early Fathers.* Some of them do employ terms which would imply, if interpreted literally, that baptism and re-generation were the same thing. But the reason of this is obvious. The Jews were accustomed to call the converts to their religion from the Gentiles, *little children,* and their introduction into the Jewish Church, a *new birth,* because they were brought, as it were, into a *new moral world.* Accordingly, circumcision is re-peatedly called in Scripture *"the covenant,"* because it was the *sign* of the covenant. Afterwards, when baptism, as a Christian ordinance, became identified with the reception of the Gospel, the early writers and preachers began to call this ordinance *regeneration,* and sometimes *illumination,* because every *adult* who was baptized, professed to be born of God, illuminated by the Holy Spirit. By a common figure of speech, they called the *sign* by the name of the *thing signified.* In the truly primitive times this language was harmless, and well understood: but as superstition increased, it gradually led to mischievous error, and became the parent of complicated and deplorable delusions.

II. But there is another view of the doctrine of baptismal regeneration, which is sometimes taken, and which, though less pernicious than that which has been examined, is still, I apprehend, fitted to mislead, and, of course, to do essential mischief. It is this: That baptism is that rite which marks and ratifies the introduction of its subject into the visible kingdom of Christ; that in this ordinance the baptized person is brought into a new state or relation to Christ, and His sacred family; and that this new state or relation is designated in Scripture by the term *regeneration,* being intended to express an *ecclesiastical birth,* that is, being "born" into the visible kingdom of the Redeemer. Those who entertain this opinion do not deny, that there is a great moral change, wrought by the Spirit of God, which must pass upon every one, before he can be in a state of salvation. This they call *conversion, renovation,* &c.; but they tell us that the term *"regeneration"* ought not to be applied to this spiritual change; that it ought to be confined to that change of *state* and of *relation* to the *visible kingdom of Christ* which is constituted by baptism; so that a person, according to them, may be regenerated, that is, regularly introduced into the visible Church, without being really born of the Spirit. This theory, though by no means so fatal in its tendency as the preceding, still appears to me liable to the following serious objections.

1. It makes an unauthorized use of an important theological term. It is vain to say, that, after giving fair notice of the *sense* in which we use a term, no misapprehension or harm can result

from the constant use of it in that sense. The plea is insufficient. If the sense in question be an unusual, and especially an unscriptural one, no one can estimate the mischief which may result from the use of it in that sense. *Names* are so closely connected with *things,* that it is of the utmost importance to preserve the nomenclature of theology from perversion and abuse. If the sense of the word "regeneration" which is embraced in this theory, were now by common consent admitted, it would give an entirely new aspect to all those passages of Scripture in which either regeneration or baptism is mentioned, making some of them unmeaning, and others ridiculous; and render unintelligible, and in a great measure useless, if not delusive, nine-tenths of the best works on the subject of practical religion that have ever been written.

2. But there is a more serious objection. If men be told that every one who is baptized, is thereby regenerated – "born of God," – "born of the Spirit," – made a "new creature in Christ," – will not the mass of mankind, in spite of every precaution and explanation that can be employed, be likely to mistake on a fundamental point; to imagine that the disease of our nature is trivial, and that a trivial remedy for it will answer; to lay more stress than they ought upon an external rite; and to make a much lower estimate than they ought of the nature and necessity of that holiness without which no man shall see the Lord?

After all, however, although the doctrine of baptismal regeneration, in the first and most objectionable sense, is known to be rejected by all the truly evangelical divines of the Church of England, and by the same class in the Protestant Episcopal Church in this country; yet it cannot be denied that something, to say the least, very like this doctrine is embodied in the baptismal service of that denomination on both sides of the Atlantic. The following specimens of its language will at once illustrate and confirm my meaning: "Seeing now, dearly beloved brethren, that *this child is regenerate, and grafted into the body of Christ's church,* let us give thanks unto Almighty God for these benefits, and with one accord make our prayers unto him, that this child may lead the rest of his life according to this beginning." And again: "We yield thee hearty thanks, most merciful Father, that it hath pleased thee to *regenerate this infant by thy Holy Spirit,* to receive him for thine own child by adoption, and to incorporate him into thy holy church," &c. The same language is also repeated in the baptismal service for "those of riper years." They are represented as being "regenerated;" as being "born again," and "made heirs of salvation;" and as having "put on Christ." This language is differently interpreted, by the Episcopal ministers who employ it, according to the opinion which they adopt with regard to baptism. Those who coincide in opinion with Bishop Mant, and others of similar sentiments, make no scruple of avowing, that these expressions literally import, what they fully believe, that every one who is duly baptized, is, in and by that rite, born of the Spirit, and brought into a state of grace and salvation. A second class of interpreters, however, consider this language of the liturgy as merely importing that the person baptized is brought into a new state, or a new relation to the visible Church. While a third class, although they, acknowledge that the language before us, literally interpreted, does certainly express more than a mere visible relation, even the participation of truly spiritual and saving blessings; yet say, that they can conscientiously employ it, because a liturgy intended for general use, ought to be, and must be, constructed upon the principle, that those who come to receive its offices are all to be considered as *sincere,* and as having a *right,* in the sight of God, to the ordinance for which they apply! And thus it happens, that those who reject as Popish and delusive, the doctrine of baptismal regeneration, as taught by Mant, and those who concur with him, feel no difficulty in publicly and solemnly repeating this language, every time they administer the ordinance of baptism.

It is not for one of another communion to interpose between the consciences of Episcopal ministers, and the import of their public formularies. In fidelity to my own principles, however, and as a warning to those of my own church who may be assailed by the proselyting efforts of some of this denomination, I may be permitted to say, that if I believed with Bishop Mant, and

his associates in sentiment, the language of the baptismal service
would be entirely to my taste; but if not, I could not, on any account, conscientiously employ it. It would not satisfy me to be
told, that the language of one of the Thirty-nine Articles, and
some of the language found in the Book of Homilies, bears a
different aspect. This is, no doubt, true. Still this does not remove
or alter the language of the baptismal service. There it stands, a
distress and a snare to thousands of good men, who acknowledge
that they could wish it otherwise, but dare not modify it in the
smallest jot or tittle.[2] Had I no other objection to ministering in
the Church of England, or in the corresponding denomination in
this country – this part of the liturgy would alone be an insurmountable one. I could not consent continually to employ language, which, however explained or counteracted, is so directly
adapted to deceive in a most vital point of practical religion. I
could not allow myself to sanction by adoption and use, language
which, however explained and counteracted in my own ministry,
I knew to be presented and urged by many around me in its literal
import, and declared to be the only true doctrine of the Church.

As to the plea, that a liturgy must necessarily be constructed upon the principle that all who come to its offices must
be *presumed* to be *sincere,* and be solemnly *assured,* in the name
of God, that they are so, nothing can be more delusive. Cannot
scriptural truth be as plainly stated, and as wisely guarded in a
liturgical composition as in any other? Our Methodist brethren
have a prescribed form for baptism; and so far as I recollect its
language, they have succeeded, without apparent difficulty, in
making it at once instructive, solemn, appropriate, and unexceptionable. And I have heard Presbyterian ministers a thousand
times tell their hearers, with as much distinctness in administering
sacraments, as in ordinary preaching, that "the sacraments be-

---

2. An evangelical and deeply conscientious minister of the Episcopal
Church, who, after struggling for some time with the most distressing scru-
ples, as to this very feature in the baptismal service, ventured to alter a few
words, was forthwith, by his diocesan, dismissed from the ministry.

come effectual to salvation, not from any virtue in them, or in him
that doth administer them; but only by the blessing of Christ, and
the working of his Spirit *in them that by faith receive them.*"

But it may be asked, what kind or degree of *efficacy do*
Presbyterians consider as connected with baptism? Do they suppose that there is any beneficial influence, physical or moral, in *all
cases,* connected with the due administration of this sacrament?
I answer, *none at all.* They suppose that the washing with water
in this ordinance is an *emblem* and a *sign* of precious benefits;
that it holds forth certain great truths, which are the glory of the
Christian covenant, and the joy of the Christian's heart; that it is
a seal affixed by God to His covenant with His people, whereby
He certifies His purposes of grace, and pledges His blessing to all
who receive it with a living faith; nay, that it is the seal of valu-
able *outward privileges,* even to those who are not then, or at any
other time, "born of the Spirit;" that, as a solemn rite appointed
by Christ, it is adapted to make a solemn impression on the serious mind but that when it is administered to the persons, or the
offspring of those who are entirely destitute of faith, there is no
pledge or certainty that it will be accompanied with *any blessing.*
They receive the *water,* but not the *Spirit.* They are engrafted into
the visible Church, but not into the spiritual Body of Christ, and
are, *after* baptism, just as they were *before,* like Simon the Sor-
cerer, "in the gall of bitterness and in the bond of iniquity."

APPENDIX THREE

Sponsors in Baptism

It is well known that the Presbyterian Church differs from the Episcopal in regard to the subject announced at the head of this note. We differ in two respects. *First,* in not requiring or encouraging the appearance of any other sponsors, in the baptism of *children,* than the *parents,* when they are living and qualified to present themselves in this character: and, *secondly,* in not requiring, or even admitting any sponsors at all in cases of *adult* baptism. My object in the remarks which I am about to make on this subject, is, not to impugn either the principles or practice of our Episcopal brethren; but simply to state, for the instruction of the members of our own church, why we cannot think or act with them in relation to this matter.

It is curious to observe the several steps by which the use of sponsors, as now established in the Romish and some Protestant churches, reached its present form. Within the first five or six hundred years after Christ, there is no evidence that children were *ever* presented for baptism by any other persons than their *parents,* provided those parents were living, and were professing Christians. When some persons, in the time of Augustine, who flourished toward the close of the *fourth,* and beginning of the *fifth* century, contended that it was not lawful, in any case, for any excepting their natural parents to offer children in baptism; that learned and pious Father opposed them, and gave it as his opinion, that, in *extraordinary cases,* as, for example, when the parents were *dead;* when they were not professing Christians; when they cruelly forsook and exposed their offspring; and when masters had young slaves committed to their charge; in these cases (and the pious Father mentions no others), he maintains that any professing Christians, who should be willing to undertake the benevolent charge, might, with propriety, take these children, offer them in baptism, and become responsible for their Christian education. This, every one will perceive, is in strict conformity with the principles maintained in the foregoing essay, and with the doctrine and habits of the Presbyterian Church.

The learned Bingham, an Episcopal divine of great learning, seems to have taken unwearied pains, in his *Ecclesiastical Antiquities*, to collect every scrap of testimony within his reach, in favour of the early origin of sponsors. But he utterly fails of producing even plausible evidence to that amount; and at length candidly acknowledges that in the early ages, *parents* were, in all ordinary cases, the presenters and sureties for their own children; and that children were presented by others only in *extraordinary* cases, such as those already alluded to. It is true, indeed, that some writers, more sanguine than discriminating, have quoted Dionysius, Tertullian, and Cyril of Alexandria, as affording countenance to the use of sponsors in early times. Not one of those writers, however, has written a sentence which favours the use of any other sponsors than parents, when they were in life, and of a proper character to offer their children for the sacramental seal in question. Even Dionysius, whose language has, at first view, some appearance of favouring such sponsors; yet, when carefully examined, will be found to speak only of sponsors who undertook to train up in the Christian religion some of the children of Pagans, who were delivered, for this purpose, into the hands of these benevolent sureties, by their unbelieving parents. But this, surely, is not inconsistent with what has been said. And, after all, the writings of this very Dionysius are given up by the learned Wall, and by the still more learned and illustrious Archbishop Usher, as a "gross and impudent forgery," unworthy of the least credit.

It was not until the council of Mentz, in the ninth century, that the Church of Rome forbade the appearance of parents as sponsors for their own children, and required that this service be surrendered to other hands.

Mention is made, by Cyril, in the *fifth* century, and by Fulgentius in the *sixth,* of sponsors in some peculiar cases of *adult* baptism. When adults, about to be baptized, were *dumb,* or under the power of *delirium,* through disease, and of course unable to speak for themselves, or to make the usual profession; in such cases it was customary for some friend or friends to answer for them, and to bear testimony to their good character, and to the fact of their having before expressed a desire to be baptized. For this, there was, undoubtedly, some reason; and the same thing might, with propriety, in conceivable circumstances be done now. From this, however, there was a transition soon made to the use of sponsors in *all cases* of adult baptism. This latter, however, was upon a different principle from the former. When adults had the gifts of speech and reason, and were able to answer for themselves, the sponsors provided for such never answered or professed for them. This was invariably done by the adult himself. Their only business, as it would appear, was to be a kind of curators or guardians of the spiritual life of the persons baptized. This office was generally fulfilled, in each church, by the *deacons,* when adult *males* were baptized; and by the *deaconesses,* when *females* came forward to receive this ordinance.

Among the pious Waldenses and Albigenses, in the middle ages, no other sponsors than parents seem to have been in common use. In one of their catechisms, as preserved by Perrin, and Morland, they ask, "By whom ought children to be presented in baptism?" Answer, "By their parents, or by any others who may be inspired with this charity;" which is evidently intended to mean, as other documents respecting them show, that where the parents were dead, or absent, or could not act, other pious professors of religion might take their places.

According to one of the canons of the Church of England, "parents are not to be *urged* to be *present* when their children are baptized, nor to be *permitted* to stand as sponsors for their own children." In the Protestant Episcopal Church in this country, parents "may be admitted as sponsors if it be desired." But in both countries it is required that there be sponsors for all adults, as well as for infants.

The baptismal service of the Methodist Church in the United States, for infants, does not recognise the use of any sponsors at all, excepting the parents, or whatever other "friends" may present them.

It is plain, then, that the early history of the Church, as well as the Word of God, abundantly sustains the doctrine and practice of the Presbyterian Church in this matter. We maintain, that as the right of the children of believers to baptism, flows from the membership and faith of their parents according to the flesh; so those parents, if living, are the only proper persons to present them for the reception of this covenant seal. If, however, their proper parents, on any account, cannot do this, they may, upon our principles, with propriety, be presented by any professed believers, who, *quoad hoc,* adopt them as their children, and are willing to engage, as parents, to "bring them up in the nurture and admonition of the Lord."

If, indeed, nothing else were contended for in this case, than that when believing parents have pious and peculiar friends who are willing to unite with them in engagements to educate their children in the true religion, such *friends* might be permitted to stand with them; there might not be so much to condemn. Even then the solemn question might be asked: "Who hath required this at your hands?" But when the system is, to set aside parents; to require that others take their places, and make engagements which *they* alone, for the most part, are qualified to make; and when, in pursuance of this system, thousands are daily making engagements which they never think of fulfilling, and in most cases, notoriously have it not in their power to fulfill, and, indeed, feel no special obligation to fulfill; we are constrained to regard it as a human invention, having no warrant whatever, either, from the Word of God or primitive usage; and as adapted, on a variety of accounts, to generate evil, much evil, rather than good.

APPENDIX FOUR

Confirmation

In the Apostolic Church, there was no such rite as that which under this name has been long established in the Romish communion as a sacrament, and adopted in some Protestant churches as a solemnity, in their view, if not commanded, yet as both expressive and edifying. It is not intended in this note to record a sentence condemnatory of those who think proper to employ the rite in question: but only to state with brevity some of the reasons why the fathers of the Presbyterian Church thought proper to exclude it from their ritual; and why their sons, to the present hour, have persisted in the same course.

1. We find no foundation for this rite in the Word of God. Indeed our Episcopal brethren, and other Protestants who employ it, do not pretend to find any direct warrant for it in Scripture. All they have to allege, which bears the least resemblance to any such practice, is the statement recorded in Acts viii. 14-17: "Now when the Apostles, which were at Jerusalem, heard that Samaria had received the Word of God, they sent unto them Peter and John, who when they were come down, prayed for them, that they might receive the Holy Ghost. (For as yet he was fallen upon none of them; only they were baptized in the name of the Lord Jesus.) Then laid they their hands on them, and they received the Holy Ghost." That there is here a reference to the *extraordinary* or *miraculous* gifts of the Holy Ghost, and these conferred by extraordinary officers, is so perfectly apparent, that it is no won-

der the advocates of Confirmation do not press it as *proof* of their point. The only wonder is, that they ever mention it as affording the most remote countenance to their practice. The diligent reader of Scripture will find *four* kinds, or occasions of laying on hands recounted in the New Testament. The first, by Christ Himself, to express an authoritative benediction, Matt. xix. Mark x. 16; the second, in the healing of diseases, Mark xvi. 18. Acts xxviii. 8; the third, in conferring the extraordinary gifts of the Spirit, Acts viii. 17. xix. 6; and the fourth, in setting apart persons to sacred office, Acts vi. 6. xiii. 3. 1 Tim. iv. 14. The venerable Dr. Owen, in his commentary on Heb. vi. 2, expresses the opinion, that the laying on of hands there spoken of, is to be considered as belonging to the third class of cases, and, of course, as referring to the extraordinary gifts of the Holy Spirit. Others have supposed that it rather belongs to the fourth example above enumerated, and therefore applies to the ordination of ministers. But there is not a syllable or hint in the whole New Testament which looks like such a laying on of hands as that for which the advocates of Confirmation contend.

2. Quite as little support for Confirmation can be found in the purest and best periods of uninspired antiquity. Towards the close of the second century, several uncommanded and superstitious additions had been made to the ordinance of baptism. Among these were anointing with *oil,* in avowed imitation of the Jewish manner of consecration; administering to the baptized individual a mixture of *milk* and *honey,* as the symbol of his childhood in a new life, and as a pledge of that heavenly Canaan, with all its advantages and happiness, to which the hopes of the baptized were directed; the *laying on of the hands* of the minister officiating in baptism, for imparting the Holy Spirit; to all which may be added, that immediately after the close of this century, we find the practice of *exorcism* introduced as a preliminary to baptism, and as a means of expelling all evil spirits from the candidate for this ordinance. These superstitious additions were made to succeed each other in the following order; *exorcism*, confession; renunciation; baptism; *chrismation*, or anointing with oil, which

was done in the form of a *cross;* and finally, the laying on of hands, or *confirmation,* which immediately followed the anointing with oil, and the administration of the simple element above mentioned. "As soon as we are baptized," says Tertullian, "we are anointed with the blessed unction." And he adds, "This unction is according to the Jewish dispensation, wherein the high priest was anointed with oil out of a horn." The laying on of hands, or confirmation, immediately followed the unction. "As soon as we come from the baptismal laver," says Tertullian, "We are anointed, and then hands are imposed." This was considered as essential to the completion of the ordinance. "We do not receive the Holy Ghost," says the same father, "in baptism, but being purified by the water, we are prepared for the Holy Ghost, and at the laying on of hands, the soul is illuminated by the Spirit." The exorcism, then, the anointing with oil, the sign of the cross, the imposition of hands for conveying the Holy Spirit, and the administration of milk and honey to the candidate, were all human additions to baptism, which came in about the same time, and ought, in our opinion, to be regarded very much in the same light with a great variety of other additions to the institutions of Christ, which, though well meant, and not destitute of expressiveness, are yet wholly unauthorized by the King and Head of the Church.

3. When the practice of the laying on of hands, as an ordinary part of the baptismal service, was added, by human invention, to that ordinance, it always *immediately followed* the application of water, and the anointing with oil. "As soon as we come from the baptismal laver," says Tertullian, "we are anointed, and then hands are laid on." And it is further acknowledged by all, that every one who was competent to baptize, was equally competent to lay on hands. The two things always went together; or rather formed parts of the baptismal ordinance, which was not thought to be consummated without the imposition of hands by him who had applied the water and the unction. And this continued to be the case throughout the greater part of the Church for the first three hundred years. Then the term *bishop* signified the pastor or overseer of a flock or congregation. Every pastor was

a bishop, as had been the case in Apostolic times. And then, in ordinary cases, none but the bishop, or pastor of each church, administered baptism. Of course, he only laid on hands. But afterwards, in the progress of corruption, when Prelacy was gradually brought in, it became customary, for the sake of doing greater honour to the prelates, to reserve this imposition of hands to them, as a part of their official prerogative. *Jerome* expressly declares, that the committing this benediction wholly to the bishops, was done "rather in honour of the priesthood, than from necessity imposed by any law" (*Dialog. Adv. Lucifer*). Even now, throughout the Greek Church, this rite is administered, for the most part, in close connection with baptism, and is dispensed by any priest who is empowered to baptize. In like manner, in the Lutheran and other German churches, in which confirmation is retained, it is administered by every pastor. Still, even when confined to prelates, this imposition of hands was not, in ordinary cases, long separated from the baptism: for the children were commonly carried to the bishop to have his hands laid upon them as soon as convenient. After a while, however, it became customary to separate the two things much more widely. Confirmation, or the laying on of the bishop's hands, began to be postponed for a number of years, according to circumstances; until, at length, it was often left till the arrival of adult age, and even, in some cases, till the decline of life. All these progressive steps evidently marked a mere human invention, for which there is no divine appointment or warrant whatever.

4. The rite of confirmation is *superfluous.* As it was plainly a human invention, so it is *unnecessary,* and answers no purpose which is not quite as well, to say the least, provided for in the Presbyterian Church, which rejects it. Is it said to be desirable that there should be some transaction or solemnity by which young people who have been baptized in their infancy, may be called to recognize their religious obligations, and, as it were, to take upon themselves the profession and the vows made on their behalf in baptism? Granted. There can be no doubt that such a solemnity is both reasonable in itself, and edifying in its tendency.

But have we not just such a solemnity in the Lord's Supper; an ordinance divinely instituted; an ordinance on which all are *qualified* to attend, and *ought* to attend, who are qualified to take on themselves, in any scriptural or rational sense, their baptismal obligations; an ordinance, in fact, specifically intended, among other things, to answer this very purpose, viz, the purpose of making a personal acknowledgment and profession of the truth, the service, and the hopes of Christ: – have we not, I say, in the Sacramental Supper just such a solemnity as we need for the end in question – simple, rational, scriptural, and to which all our children may come, just as soon as they are prepared in any form to confess Christ before men? We do not *need* confirmation, then, for the purpose for which it is professed to be desired. We have something better, because appointed of God; quite as expressive; more solemn; and free from certain objectionable features which are now to be mentioned.

5. Finally; we reject the rite of confirmation in our church, because, in addition to all the reasons which have been mentioned, we consider the formula prescribed for its administration in the Church of England, and substantially adopted by the Episcopal Church in this country, as liable to the most serious objections. We do not think it a duty in any form, to practise a rite which the Saviour never appointed; but our repugnance is greatly increased by the language with which the rite in question is administered by those who employ it. In the "Order of Confirmation," as prescribed and used in the Protestant Episcopal Church in the United States, the following language occurs. Before the act of laying on hands, the officiating bishop, in his prayer, repeats the following language: "Almighty and ever living God, who hast vouchsafed *to regenerate these thy servants, by water and the* HOLY GHOST, and hast given unto them forgiveness of all their sins," &c. &c. And again, in another prayer, after the act of confirmation is completed, he speaks to the Searcher of hearts thus: "We make our humble supplications unto thee for these thy servants, upon whom, after the example of thy holy Apostles, we have now laid our hands; to *certify them by this sign of thy fa-*

vour and gracious goodness towards them," &c. And also, in the
act of laying on hands, assuming that all who are kneeling before
him *already have* the holy sanctifying Spirit of Christ, he prays
that they "may all daily *increase* in this Holy Spirit more and
more."

Such is the language addressed to large circles of young
people of both sexes, many of whom, there is every reason to
fear, are very far from having been "born of the Spirit" in the
Bible sense of that phrase; nay, some of whom manifest so little
seriousness, that any pastor of enlightened piety would be pained
to see them at a communion table yet the bishop pronounces
them *all – and* he appeals to heaven for the truth of his sentence
– he pronounces them *all* regenerate, not only by *water,* but also
by the HOLY GHOST; *certifies* to them, in the name of God, that
they are objects of the divine *"favour;"* and declares that, being
already in a state of grace and favour with God, they are called
to "grow in grace;" to "increase in the Holy Spirit more and
more."

There are many who have long regarded, and who now
regard this language not only with regret, but with shuddering! as
adapted to cherish false hopes, nay, to deceive and destroy souls
by wholesale! I must again say, that if there were no other obsta-
cle to my consenting to minister in the Protestant Episcopal
Church, *this* alone would be an insurmountable one. For it must
come home to the conscience and the feelings, not of the bishop
only, but of every pastor in that church who has, from time to
time, a circle of beloved youth to present for confirmation. It is
vain to say, that the church *presumes* that all who come are sincere, and of course born of the Spirit, and in a state of favour
with God. This is the very point of objection. She so presumes,
and undertakes to *"certify"* them of it. Presbyterian ministers do
not, dare not, use such language. They do not, and dare not, undertake to "certify" to any number of the most mature and exemplary communicants that ever gathered round a sacramental table,
that they are *all* in a state of grace and salvation, and that they
have nothing to do but to "follow on," and "increase in the Holy

Spirit." Nor is it a sufficient answer, I repeat, to say, that a liturgy, being a fixed composition, cannot be so constructed as to discriminate between different characters. This is denied. Every enlightened and faithful minister, of whatever denomination, who is at liberty to employ such language as he approves, knows how to express himself, both in prayer and preaching, in discriminating and impressive terms; and how to avoid modes of expression adapted to deceive and betray unwary souls. It is surely not impracticable to address the largest and most promiscuous assembly in a manner which, though not adapted to the precise case of every individual, shall be at least free from error, free from every thing of a deceptive and ensnaring character. Our Methodist brethren, it was before remarked, have a prescribed liturgical form for baptism; which they have rendered sufficiently discriminating, and at the same time unexceptionably safe. And, what is not unworthy of notice in this place, though the liturgy of the Protestant Episcopal Church is evidently the model which, to a certain extent, they have kept before them in constructing their own, they have wisely discarded altogether the ceremony of confirmation from their ritual.

The advocates of confirmation, as a separate ecclesiastical rite, seldom fail of quoting Calvin as expressing an opinion decisively in favour of it. This is doing great injustice to that illustrious man. Calvin directly and warmly opposes the idea of confirmation being considered as a distinct ordinance, claiming divine authority in the Church of God. This he reprobates; and especially the practice of confining the administration of it to prelates; but adds, that he has no objection to parents bringing their children to their minister, at the close of childhood, or the commencement of adolescence, to be examined according to the catechism in common use, and then, for the sake of greater dignity and reverence, closing the ceremony by the imposition of hands. "Such imposition of hands, therefore, says he, *as is simply connected with benediction,* I highly approve, and wish it were now restored to its primitive use, uncorrupted by superstition" (*Institutiones,* Lib. iv. chap. xix. § 4). But what serves to throw light on Calvin's real sentiments on this whole subject is that, in commenting on Acts viii. 17, he reproaches the Papists for pressing that passage into the support of their sacrament of confirmation; and not only asserts, but proves, that the laying on of hands there spoken of, relates, not at all to the ordinary and sanctifying, but to the miraculous gifts of the Holy Ghost, which have long since ceased in the Church; and, of course, that the passage in question ought never to be quoted in favour of confirmation, or of any other permanent rite in the Christian Church.

APPENDIX FIVE

Vote of the Westminster Assembly Respecting Baptism

It has been sometimes ignorantly, and most erroneously asserted, that the Westminster Assembly of divines, in putting to vote whether baptism should be performed by *sprinkling* or *immersion,* carried it in favour of *sprinkling,* by a majority of *one only.* This is wholly incorrect. The facts were these. When the committee who had been charged with preparing a "Directory for the Worship of God," brought in their report, they had spoken of the *mode* of baptism thus: *"It is lawful and sufficient to sprinkle the child."* To this Dr. Lightfoot, among others, objected; not because he doubted of the entire sufficiency of sprinkling – for he decidedly *preferred* sprinkling to immersion – but because he thought there was an impropriety in pronouncing that mode *lawful* only, when no one present had any doubts of its being so, and when almost all preferred it. Others seemed to think, that by saying nothing about *dipping,* that mode was meant to be *excluded,* as not a *lawful* mode. This they did not wish to pronounce. When, therefore, the clause, as originally reported, was put to vote, there were twenty-five votes in favour of it, and twenty-four against it. After this vote, a motion was made and carried, that it be *recommitted.* The next day, when the committee reported, and when some of the members still seemed unwilling to exclude all mention of *dipping,* Dr. Lightfoot remarked, that to say that *pouring* or *sprinkling* was *lawful,* would be "all one as

151

saying, that it was *lawful* to use *bread and wine* in the Lord's Supper." He, therefore, moved that the clause in the "Directory" respecting the mode of baptism, be expressed thus:

"Then the minister is to demand the name of the child, which being told him, he is to say (calling the child by his name): *'I baptize thee in the name of the Father, and of the Son, and of the Holy Ghost.'*

"As he pronounceth these words, he is to baptize the child with water, which, for the manner of doing it, is not only *lawful but sufficient,* and *most expedient* to be, by *pouring* or *sprinkling* of the water on the face of the child without adding any other ceremony." This was carried. See Lightfoot's *Life,* prefixed to the first volume of his *Works* (folio edition), p. 4; compared with Neal's *History of the Puritans,* Vol. II, pp. 100, 107, compared with the Appendix, No. II (quarto edition), where the *Directory,* as finally passed, is given at full length.

We do not learn, precisely, either from Lightfoot's biographer (who was no other than the indefatigable Strype), or from Neal, by what vote the clause, as moved by Lightfoot, was finally adopted; but Neal expressly tells us, that "the Directory passed the Assembly with *great unanimity.*"

From this statement, it is evident, that the question which was carried in the Assembly, by a majority of *one,* was not whether affusion or sprinkling was a *lawful* mode of baptism; but whether all mention of *dipping,* as *one* of the *lawful* modes should be *omitted.* This, in an early stage of the discussion, was carried, by a majority of one in the affirmative. But it would seem that the clause, as finally adopted, which certainly was far more decisive in favour of sprinkling or allusion, was passed "with *great unanimity.*" At any rate, nothing can be more evident than that the clause as it originally stood, being carried by one vote only, and afterwards, when recommitted, and so altered as to be *much stronger* in favour of sprinkling, and then adopted without difficulty, the common statement of this matter by our Baptist brethren is an entire misrepresentation.

Made in the USA
Columbia, SC
22 July 2024

38505760R00087